OWN
THE
WORLD

FISHER INVESTMENTS PRESS

Fisher Investments Press brings the research, analysis, and market intelligence of Fisher Investments' research team, headed by CEO and *New York Times* best-selling author Ken Fisher, to all investors. The Press will cover a range of investing and market-related topics for a wide audience—from novices to enthusiasts to professionals.

Books by Ken Fisher

The Ten Roads to Riches
The Only Three Questions That Count
100 Minds That Made the Market
The Wall Street Waltz
Super Stocks

Fisher Investments Series

Own the World
Aaron Anderson

Fisher Investments On Series

Fisher Investments on Energy
Fisher Investments on Materials

FISHER
INVESTMENTS
PRESS

Own the World

How Smart Investors Create Global Portfolios

Aaron Anderson

WILEY

John Wiley & Sons, Inc.

Published by John Wiley & Sons, Inc., Hoboken, New Jersey.

Published simultaneously in Canada.

For general information on our other products and services or for technical support, please contact our Customer Care Department within the United States at (800) 762-2974, outside the United States at (317) 572-3993 or fax (317) 572-4002.

Wiley also publishes its books in a variety of electronic formats. Some content that appears in print may not be available in electronic books. For more information about Wiley products, visit our web site at www.wiley.com.

Library of Congress Cataloging-in-Publication Data:

Anderson, Aaron, 1971-
Own the world : how smart investors create global portfolios / Aaron Anderson.
    p. cm. -- (Fisher investments series)
Includes bibliographical references and index.
ISBN 978-0-470-28538-1 (cloth)
    1. Portfolio management. 2. Investment analysis. 3. Securities. I. Title.
HG4529.5.A52 2009
332.6—dc22

2008041527

Printed in the United States of America

10 9 8 7 6 5 4 3 2 1

Contents

Preface

America is an island. Ok, it's not an island in the traditional sense. We're not surrounded by water. Inhabitants here don't live on a diet of coconuts and . . . well . . . coconuts. And it's rare to find folks in grass skirts dancing to ukulele tunes. But if you looked closely at many US investors' portfolios, you'd think we're almost completely isolated from other countries. *Own the World* is out to change all that.

We at Fisher Investments manage billions of dollars in global equities for about 25,000 clients. We believe wholeheartedly down to the marrow of our bones global is the best way to invest. That's not because foreign stocks make better investments than US stocks. Sometimes foreign stocks beat US stocks, and sometimes US stocks win. But the many benefits of global investing persist no matter which markets happen to be performing best at any given time.

Collectively, US investors own far fewer foreign stocks than they often should. This is despite the fact global investing has increased dramatically in recent years. It's estimated today about 60 percent of US equity investors have some exposure to foreign stocks. That's a big increase from a few years ago, when only about 30 percent invested overseas. So it's clear US investors are catching on to the fact global investing is both possible and beneficial, yet most are simply dipping their toes in the ocean when they should be going for a swim.

While it's true there are quite a few great investment opportunities here in America, there are also tremendous opportunities abroad. Many of the world's biggest and fastest growing companies are located outside the US, so global investing opens a world of opportunity (pun intended).

The potential for boosting performance is one important reason to warm to foreign stocks, but the possibility of better returns isn't the only reason. As you'll read, seeking to lower risk through diversification is another important attribute of a global investment portfolio. Non-US stocks don't move in lockstep with US stocks, but their aggregate long-term returns are about the same. So including foreign stocks in your portfolio can reduce volatility (or *risk* in investing parlance) without sacrificing long-term performance. That's not to say there aren't periods when US and foreign stocks move together. In many ways, a stock is still a stock, no matter where it comes from. When investors don't want to own stocks, they often don't want to own stocks from any country. As I write this in 2008, both US and foreign stocks are slogging through a global morass affecting stocks in just about every country on the planet. At times like this, when foreign stocks are suffering right alongside their US counterparts, the benefits of global investing can be difficult to see. But they're there. The same holds true when investors are clamoring to get their hands on as many shares as possible causing stock everywhere to skyrocket together.

So if stocks have a place in your portfolio (and they probably do), investing globally adds a multitude of benefits. But if stocks don't makes sense for you given your investment objectives, that prescription applies to global stock as well as domestic. Whatever asset allocation you settle on, a good long-term investing plan should take into account both good times and bad.

It would be a mistake to call *Own the World* a global investing guide. Guides typically tell you where to go. Travel guides list the best hotels, museums, and cafes in cities all over the planet. But they don't necessarily tell you *why* you should go there. As you'll read, the composition of the world's stock markets provides the best guide for investors. *Own the World* is more of a treatise explaining why you should invest globally, the tools available to global investors, and many of the things to watch out for.

Books touting specific markets to invest in are often a waste of money. They're usually written about stocks in countries that have done well in the past because many investors are interested in learning about the next hot market. But markets are dynamic, and today's hot market might be tomorrow's dud. Dozens of books were written about investing in China after Chinese stocks boomed in 2007. But already in 2008, many Chinese shares have given back most if not all of their 2007 gains. Chasing hot markets is like chasing your tail. Quite often, you end up biting yourself in the rear.

More often than not, we find clients have scant experience investing in foreign stocks prior to working with us. Many are initially apprehensive about expanding portfolios overseas, so we're continually educating clients on the many benefits a global portfolio offers. Hopefully, this book will impart some of the knowledge we've attained about global investing and the rewards and challenges that go along with it.

Acknowledgments

I can't type. Honestly. In an ill-fated decision during my high school years, I never enrolled in typing class, forever handicapping my ability to produce anything literary. Being that my shortcomings as an author begin at the most fundamental level and certainly don't end there, you can imagine how many people I leaned on heavily to write this book.

To begin, I'd like to thank Ken Fisher, Andrew Teufel, and Jeff Silk—the members of Fisher Investments' Investment Policy Committee. Their years of dedication making Fisher Investments the firm it is today provided me this opportunity. They've also kept me employed, for which I'm particularly grateful. I owe an additional debt of gratitude to Andrew for his guidance with every aspect of this book.

If anyone deserves credit for preventing this book from degrading into a meaningless heap of gobbledygook, it's Lara Hoffmans. A simple acknowledgment here isn't ample thanks for the years the stresses I've caused have undoubtedly taken off her life. Dina Ezzat and Evelyn Chea were also instrumental in making sure my i's were dotted and my t's crossed, an especially daunting task given my lack of typing skill.

Marc Haberman, Molly Lienesch, and Fabrizio Ornani deserve enormous credit, not only for their assistance with this book but for making Fisher Investments Press a reality.

The help I received from the Fisher Investments Research Team was invaluable. Particular thanks to Jennifer Chou for her research support and William Glaser for helping procure the resources needed to make this book possible. And it's quite likely I'd have gone mad if it wasn't for the encouragement I received from Michael Hanson.

Without data, all the charts, tables, and calculations herein would be nothing more than blank pages, significantly lessening their usefulness. So special thanks go out to the folks at Thomson Datastream, MSCI Inc., and Global Financial Data for providing the data for our research.

My family is deserving of endless thanks shouted from mountaintops for the support they've given me in every aspect of my life. Unfortunately, my shortcomings in mountain climbing exceed even those in typing. So until I learn to master the carabiner, they'll have to settle for heartfelt thanks here. Mom, Dad, and Kevin—thank you.

Last, I'd like to thank my beautiful wife, Kim. Without her love, support, and patience, I would never find the strength to put pen to paper.

Who Needs a Global Investment Portfolio?

Hopefully, you're not bent on world domination. If you expected to casually thumb through an imperialist manifesto, you've been led astray by the title of this book. *Own the World* has nothing to do with conquering the world—unless you're referring to the world of global investing. But even if you were hoping to overthrow a government or two, you'd be well served to read on. Maybe you'll find expanding the horizons of your investment portfolio is just as satisfying as expanding your empire. As you'll learn, it's easier, cheaper, and involves significantly less bloodshed. All you need to do is embrace the myriad opportunities to manage risk and enhance performance offered by investing globally. No shady arms deals or knowledge of military tactics required.

Global investing can involve just about any type of asset. Italian cars, French wine, Greek sculptures, Australian bonds, Canadian

1

commodities, Hong Kong real estate—all legitimate options. But "legitimate" doesn't mean appropriate. It'd be cool to sink some dough into a classic Ferrari Testarossa. But a fender bender puts a serious dent in your retirement plans. When it comes to investing, most folks should stick primarily to stocks, bonds, and cash. They're sufficiently liquid, have reasonable transaction costs, and involve measurable risks. That doesn't mean a Picasso can't provide a decent return, but few investors have the means, know-how, or appropriate facilities to make *Garçon à la Pipe* viable. If you want to sprinkle in a few more exotic investments, do so with caution. Stocks, bonds, and cash should comprise the core of most investment portfolios.

THE MOST IMPORTANT QUESTION

Stocks, bonds, or cash. But how much of each? A simple question, but vital. In fact, the answer will likely impact your returns more than any other decision. It's true. The asset class you choose is more important than anything you can learn about global investing. But even a perfect asset allocation will fall flat if you're not investing correctly. Just buying a few stocks isn't the right way to play the stock market. And owning a corporate bond or two isn't a good fixed income strategy. *Diversification* and *risk control* are essential components of any well-constructed portfolio. This book's aim is to show why global is the best way to invest, but it can't determine which asset allocation is most appropriate for you. Why? Because that decision requires a thorough analysis of your personal circumstances—namely your investment objectives, cash flow needs, and time horizon. But there are really only three major investing goals for the vast majority of people. Most want their portfolios to:

1. Grow over time.
2. Provide income.
3. Do some combination of numbers 1 and 2.

The appropriate allocation for each goal will depend on a number of considerations. But generally, if you want more growth, and have a long time horizon, hold more stocks. If you require more income, you may need some bonds or even cash. Or maybe not—depends on how much cash flow you need and your time horizon. But most folks requiring income still need some stocks.

What about risk tolerance? Shouldn't risk tolerance factor into this decision? Not without first defining *risk*. As covered in Chapter 3, *investment risk* usually means *volatility*. But there's also the risk you won't meet your investing goals. The fact investing in stocks makes some people uneasy doesn't change the fact stocks almost always have superior long-term returns.[1] As you'll read, investing globally can help mitigate some, but not all, of the volatility associated with stocks while still capturing stocks' growth potential. For most, stomaching the volatility inherent in stocks gives them the best chance of achieving their growth objectives. So unless stock market volatility is affecting the proper functioning of some of your vital organs, don't let nervousness about short-term market volatility get in the way of achieving your long-term goals. Besides, stocks might not be as risky as you think.

Stocks Are Safer

Many investors mistakenly think bonds and cash are "safe" because, near-term, they can be less volatile than stocks. If they need income, folks believe they should own few stocks if any at all. But this is usually very wrong.

Why? Stocks pretty much always outperform bonds and cash over any significantly long time period. If you look at 20-year periods throughout history, stocks trounce bonds almost every time. It isn't just US stocks; it's true of stocks in most countries. Table 1.1 compares returns on stocks versus government bonds for various countries over 20-year periods from 1926 through 2007 (i.e. 1926–1946, 1927–1947, etc. UK data starts in 1932). As you can see, stocks outperform bonds far more often than not.

Table 1.1   Stocks vs. Bonds

Country	Frequency of Stocks Outperforming Bonds	Average 20-Year Return Stocks	Bonds
US	98.4%	924.9%	243.5%
UK	100.0%	1,302.1%	432.2%
Japan	82.3%	3,066.0%	284.7%
Germany	77.4%	481.7%	196.7%

Source: Global Financial Data.

How to Win in Vegas

Not only do stocks usually outperform bonds over the long-term, they do so by a wide margin. In America, stocks' average 20-year return since 1926 beats bonds almost four to one! I hate investing-gambling analogies because there's a huge difference between the two—at least when investing correctly. But imagine walking into Caesar's Palace, and in addition to normal slot machines, blackjack, and craps tables, they offer a game paying four times your money 98 percent of the time. If that game existed, you'd play until the pit boss had to hock his watch, his home, and his first-born child. Stocks' historical long-term returns mean stocks should comprise a significant portion (if not the bulk) of most investment portfolios—unless you have a very short time horizon or zero desire for growth (i.e., probably not you). And as demonstrated in this book, if it makes sense to own stocks, it makes sense to invest globally—always. Ergo, it makes sense for virtually all investors to make global stocks a meaningful part of their portfolios.

"HOME, SWEET HOME" BIAS

Many US investors invest solely in domestic stocks. Stock ownership is the American way! Often, our preference for US stocks begins at an early age. Maybe your grandparents gave you a few stock certificates as a kid, hoping you'd become a young tycoon. But no matter when they start, most folks begin with well-known US companies.

Stocks like Coca-Cola, General Electric, General Motors, or Procter & Gamble may have comprised your fledgling portfolio instead of Toyota, British Petroleum, or Nokia.

And why shouldn't most investors' first inkling be to invest only in the US? For a long time, sticking with US stocks was probably very rational. For much of modern history, hurdles to foreign investing were relatively high—particularly for individual investors. But the investing world is changing rapidly, and the majority of these hurdles have toppled like the Berlin Wall, making foreign investing easier than ever.

Where Has Global Investing Been?

You may have heard investing outside the US is difficult, time consuming, and requires special skills and experience attainable only by hacking through foreign jungles with a machete. Some of that may have been true in the past, but global investing has changed dramatically in recent years. Today, foreign investing is barely more difficult than investing in US companies.

Many mature markets have been open to foreign investors for years—make that centuries. The Dutch East India Company first tapped investment dollars by listing shares on the Amsterdam Stock Exchange in 1602. But equity market liberalization in many places is relatively new. Capital markets in many countries are still developing, and some countries place significant restrictions on foreign investing. But even investing in countries welcoming foreign investors has involved a number of challenges.

Getting the 411.   Getting your hands on information about foreign markets was difficult. Since the first ticker tape machines tapped out stock prices in the late nineteenth century, information about stocks listed on US exchanges has been relatively easy to obtain. But foreign stocks were a different story. Pricing information wasn't timely. Accounting standards weren't uniform. Press releases and earnings announcements often weren't translated into English. Foreign news sources weren't readily available. As a result, getting up-to-date, accurate information about foreign markets meant speaking a dozen different languages and even traveling the globe looking for investing opportunities.

Border Patrol.   There were also few vehicles enabling US investors to easily invest abroad. In 1990, only 122 mutual funds deemed "global" or "international" (more on that dreaded word shortly) were available in the US.[2] Exchange-traded funds (ETFs) didn't even exist in the US until the mid-1990s. And buying foreign shares not traded on US exchanges usually required establishing accounts with foreign brokerage firms which could be onerous and costly. Some institutional investors weren't even allowed to invest overseas because they perceived foreign investing as not only risky, but unpatriotic!

Global Markets Are Now Open for Business

The current environment is much different. Most countries have realized the benefits of opening their markets to foreign investors. Foreign companies benefit because availing themselves to the large pool of global capital can reduce the cost of raising money. If more investors are interested in investing in a firm, it can usually raise money at more favorable terms. Additionally, global investors often provide technology and expertise to firms that need them. These realizations led many formerly closed markets to embrace global investors with open arms.

We now have better access to information about foreign economies, markets, and companies, thanks largely to the Internet. For those with a modicum of computer savvy, information on foreign countries and stocks is a mouse click away. Foreign firms provide financial information, annual reports, press releases, and a host of other relevant information right on their websites. If you prefer the ink and pulp medium of newspapers, you can have any number of foreign newspapers delivered to your door. As an added bonus for those who don't speak Farsi, these are usually translated into English. Foreign executives are wise to the fact that the more people who can read about their firms, the more foreign investors they're likely to attract.

There are also more ways to invest abroad than ever. There are now thousands of foreign investments easily available to US investors. Chapter 7 looks at some of these in greater detail. And global exchanges are integrating at a rapid pace, so investors have much greater access to investments on exchanges around the world. In 2006, the NYSE Group, operator of the New York Stock Exchange, merged with Euronext N.V., one of Europe's largest exchanges, to form NYSE Euronext. In 2007, the London Stock Exchange merged with the Borsa Italiana S.p.A., Italy's primary exchange. In 2008, the NASDAQ Exchange merged with OMX AB, which operates exchanges in Nordic and Baltic countries, to form the NASDAQ OMX Group. Incidentally, Borse Dubai, operator of the two main exchanges in the United Arab Emirates, holds significant stakes in both the NASDAQ OMX Group and the London Stock Exchange. These are just a few examples of the wave of mergers and partnerships among global exchanges. All this integration means investors can more easily buy and sell stocks in far-off lands.

We Still Don't Get It

Despite the increased ease of foreign investing, US investors remain woefully underexposed to foreign stocks, as shown in Figure 1.1, which illustrates US investors' total foreign equity ownership.

US investors in aggregate have over $21 trillion invested in stocks,[3] but only $4.8 trillion, or 22 percent, is allocated to foreign stocks.[4] This is a significant increase from just a few years ago, but still far from reflecting the composition of global equity markets.

A more detailed description of the global landscape is forthcoming in Chapter 4, but the value of US stocks comprises less than 50 percent of all tradable stocks in the world. Less than half—that's it! Don't put away your red, white, and blue "We're #1" foam finger just yet. The next biggest market, currently Britain, is less than one quarter the size of the US. In fact, you'd have to combine all the stocks in the next 10 largest countries to equal the market capitalization of the US.[5] We're not only number one—we're number one by a huge margin.

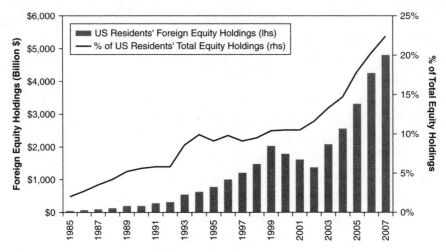

Figure 1.1   US Investors' Foreign Allocation
Source: US Department of the Treasury.

As such, US stocks should play a prominent role in both US and non-US investors' portfolios. But the optimal mix of foreign and domestic stocks should be driven by the market capitalizations of the countries making up the world. In other words, if America is 45 percent of the world stock market value, Britain 11 percent, and Djibouti 0.00003 percent, you should generally hold about 45 percent US stocks, 11 percent UK, and 0.00003 percent Djibouti (that is, if you find a Djibouti stock—if not, you can easily skip Djibouti).

You needn't rigidly adhere to this mix. If you're not so optimistic about US stocks, you might put less than 45 percent in the US. Or, if you think the US will do great, you might own more than 45 percent here. Later chapters will show that a number of different strategies or factors might cause you to include more or less of certain countries. But the relative sizes of stock markets in each country should serve as a starting point.

Believe it or not, foreign investors need global diversification even more than we do in the US. As an American, half of your portfolio in your home country is still a sizable portion. But imagine a British investor trying to properly diversify globally. A Brit would invest only 10 percent or so of his portfolio at home. And the UK is the second largest market! Investors in smaller markets need to send even greater portions of their portfolios abroad. It might seem difficult, but it's the right thing to do.

If investors around the world were properly diversified, US investors would only own about 45 percent of US stocks and non-US investors would own the rest. Yet we collectively own far more. So not only do we own too many US stocks, but foreigners own too few! A preference for stocks in our home country isn't a trait exclusive to US investors. Investors in most countries usually keep more of their portfolios at home than they should. This is commonly referred to as *home bias*.

It's a universal truth—biases are bad in investing, and a home bias is no exception. Any investment decision based on your political leanings, sports teams, favorite color, or astrological sign will undoubtedly cause you to overlook great investment options elsewhere. Do yourself a favor: Keep biases far, far away from your investment portfolio. They can cost you. So what causes this home bias?

Definition

Home Bias

Home bias is the tendency for investors to favor stocks in their home countries. A US investor owning mostly US stocks has a home bias toward the US. Same with a French investor owning mostly French stocks, a Portuguese investor owning mostly Portuguese stocks, an Aussie favoring Australian stocks, and so on.

Dreaming of Far Away Places

Many factors shape our preference for domestic stocks. One of the most fundamental factors is our perception of foreign countries. When many investors think about things foreign, investing isn't their focus. What do you think of when your mind wanders to foreign environs? Is it that trip to Europe you took after college, lugging your backpack from hostel to hostel, soaking up the culture all the while trying to figure out how to order a Big Mac in German? Or is it your honeymoon in Tahiti, sipping fruity cocktails on the beach, concerned only about the adequacy of your sunscreen's SPF? Unless you travel abroad regularly for work, your perception is probably that foreign lands are romantic and leisurely. On trips overseas, we're trying to put the stresses of everyday life behind us and enjoy the relaxed side of life. Worries about sales figures, paradigm shifts, out-of-the-box thinking, and action items are reserved for the US of A.

Or you may have the opposite opinion of foreign countries. Often, our view of foreign lands is shaped by the snippets we see on TV or read about in the paper, and they can be less than glowing. As a result, you might see foreign countries as places where most drivers are on the wrong side of the road and the water isn't safe to drink.

Close your eyes and think of France. Do you see the Eiffel Tower and the Arc de Triomphe or the home of the world's largest utility? Does the UK make you think of Buckingham Palace or global banking behemoths financing infrastructure projects in emerging markets? Is South Korea a country in a continual standoff with its neighbor to the north or the domicile of one of the world's largest electronics companies? Truth is foreign countries can be vacation spots or nightly news fodder, but they're also homes to some of the world's best firms. Yet most Americans confine their search for investment options to our borders.

Ignore Mr. Wisdom

Conventional wisdom is partly to blame. Conventional wisdom tells us somewhere between 10 and 20 percent of a US investor's portfolio should be allocated overseas because foreign is too "risky." This begs the question: Who is this Mr. Wisdom, and why is he qualified to advise you on your portfolio allocation? Wasn't it Mr. Wisdom who once said the earth was flat? Didn't Mr. Wisdom assure us humans couldn't fly?

Once again, Mr. Wisdom is leading us astray. Recommending a mere 10 percent to 20 percent allocation to foreign stocks is way out of line with global equity market make-up. Is Mr. Wisdom arbitrarily excluding an entire hemisphere? Even a bias toward companies domiciled east of the Prime Meridian or north of the equator still wouldn't result in an 80/20 allocation. Frankly, we have little respect for Mr. Wisdom's advice, especially as it pertains to investing. And this recommendation by Mr. Wisdom is no exception.

We Like What We Know

Home bias also results from investors' preference for investing in companies they know. Most US investors would rather own shares of General Electric, a well-known US industrial conglomerate, than shares of Siemens, a comparable German company. Many of us have seen and maybe even used a Caterpillar tractor, but few of us have even heard of Komatsu—a Japanese company and one of Caterpillar's main competitors. And that catchy Intel jingle warms our hearts while the thought of owning shares of Taiwan Semiconductor leaves us cold. Despite our affinity for familiar, home-grown companies, we all utilize products made by foreign companies on a daily basis—often without knowing it. (Chapter 2 covers some of the foreign goods and services many of us use every day.)

Bigger Isn't Always Better

The aforementioned grand size of US equity markets may also inhibit foreign investment. If our skies are so spacious, our plains so fruited, and our stock markets so large, why even consider looking abroad? There are so many perfectly good stocks to choose from right here! Can't you build a perfectly good, well-diversified investment portfolio of US stocks?

Believe it or not, as great as America is, the best investment options aren't always in the US. Judging by size alone, some of the world's largest stocks in a number of sectors are located abroad. By market value, the largest energy, banking, and telecommunications companies are Chinese; the largest Materials company is Australian; and the largest food company is Swiss.[6] And the landscape continues evolving. Just five years ago, 8 of the 10 largest companies in the

Table 1.2   Largest Global Stocks

Company (2003)	Country	Company (2008)	Country
General Electric	US	PetroChina	China
Microsoft	US	ExxonMobil	US
Pfizer	US	General Electric	US
ExxonMobil	US	China Mobile	Hong Kong/China
Wal-Mart Stores	US	Gazprom	Russia
Citigroup	US	ICBC	China
Johnson & Johnson	US	Microsoft	US
Royal Dutch/Shell	Netherlands	Petrobras	Brazil
BP	UK	Royal Dutch Shell	Netherlands
IBM	US	Berkshire Hathaway	US

Source: Shlomo Z. Reifman, "The Global 2000," *Forbes*, July 21, 2003; Scott DeCarlo, "The World's Biggest Companies," *Forbes*, April 2, 2008.

world were US companies.[7] As of this writing, that number was down to four. Table 1.2 shows the 10 largest companies by market value in 2003 and 2008.

Obviously, being the biggest doesn't necessarily mean they're the best, but the changing make-up of the world's largest stocks is a clear indication foreign companies have become significant, if not dominant, players on the global stage.

Mythical Multinationals

What about all those big US multinationals? Many US companies generate significant amounts of revenue overseas. In fact, as highlighted in the next chapter, some of the largest, best-known US corporations derive more sales outside the US than they do here at home. Doesn't investing in these companies give investors exposure to foreign markets?

Simply, no. Conditions where a firm is domiciled have major impacts on its stock performance. A US firm selling popsicles in Spain will benefit from a heat wave on the Iberian Peninsula. But that doesn't mean the stock will act like a Spanish stock. On the contrary, US multinationals tend to act more like US stocks than foreign stocks, even when doing significant business abroad (you'll see this illustrated in Chapter 3).

Domestic economic, market, and political conditions impact a nation's stocks no matter where they operate. For instance, changes in US capital gains tax rate don't discriminate between US-domiciled firms garnering profits primarily at home versus those operating significantly overseas. Similarly, the interest rate environment in the US impacts most US companies in one way or another. The same is true for every nation. Japanese multinationals act like Japanese stocks; Djibouti multinationals act like Djibouti stocks.

Global Investing Isn't as Scary as You Think

Arguably the most significant contributor to home bias is the all-too-common perception foreign stocks are more risky than US stocks. Investors' impression of foreign markets is punctuated by periods of well-publicized turmoil: the Mexican peso devaluation of 1994; the Southeast Asian Financials Crisis of 1997; the Russian debt default of 1998. All headline grabbers, well-chronicled in investing lore, forever contributing to our fear of foreign markets just as the *Friday the 13th* movies make us sure a trip to summer camp will involve a masked madman emerging from the nearby woods.

What didn't make headlines is that from 1994 through 2007, Mexican stocks have provided average annualized returns of 16.1 percent (versus 11.2 percent for US stocks.)[8] Since Asia recovered from its financial crisis, stocks in many Southeast Asian countries have soared. In Thailand, the epicenter of the crisis, the Stock Exchange of Thailand Index has had 15.3 percent average annual returns.[9] Indonesia's Jakarta Index has returned 20.4 percent per year, and the Philippines Kuala Lumpur Index has climbed 12.7 percent annually. These all trump annual US returns of 1.7 percent per year over the same period. And the Russian stock market, still nascent at the time of the country's debt crisis, has been booming in recent years, providing investors with average annual returns of 50.1 percent since 1998.[10]

Those markets zigged while our markets zagged. Why? Because many conditions impacting stocks in one country or region are confined to that specific area. A discussion of correlations among different countries and the impact on investment risk follows in Chapter 3, but for now, take my word for it—investing in both zigging and zagging markets is a good thing because it can actually reduce risk, which is exactly the opposite of what most investors believe.

WE'RE NOT ALONE OUT THERE

As stated earlier, inadequate global diversification isn't a US-only trait. Quite the contrary. Investors in virtually every nation have home biases to varying degrees.

At one end of the spectrum are Chinese investors. In China, government capital controls prevent virtually all citizens from buying anything but Chinese stocks. Similarly, foreign investors have limited access to Chinese shares unless they're listed outside China's mainland exchanges. Chinese investors have a state-induced home bias.

On the other end of the spectrum are the citizens of Luxembourg. Why Luxembourg? First, who doesn't love to use the ethnonym "Luxembourger"? Second, Luxembourg's market packs a disproportionately large punch for its size in terms of the total value of shares traded there. The Luxembourg Stock Exchange (or Bourse de Luxembourg for those of you who *parlez-vous français*) has 261 firms with shares listed, but only 34 are actually Luxembourg-based.[11] A single firm—steel producer Arcelor Mittal—accounts for over 70 percent of the combined market value of those 34 issues. Add the next two largest, and these three make up about 90 percent of the total value of domestic, publicly traded Luxembourgian companies. Imagine the plight of the poor Luxembourger. She can either sink her entire nest egg into these few stocks or she can look abroad for investment options. The first path leaves her with a poorly diversified portfolio, heavily weighted to a single economic sector. The second provides her with tens of thousands of companies to choose from.

The choice seems simple. But like us Yankees, Luxembourgers express a degree of home bias as well. In fact, to varying degrees, investors in virtually every country have dedicated a larger proportion of their investment dollars (or yen, pounds, or euros as the case may be) to stocks in their home countries than the composition of global equity markets would prescribe.

GLOBAL ISN'T INTERNATIONAL

More and more investors and investment advisors are catching on to the benefits of global investing, but few get it right. There's a lot more to global investing than buying a few stocks with an *ñ* or *ü* in the name. Many even get the terminology wrong by equating "international" investing with "global" investing. By definition, if something is *international,* it involves multiple countries but not necessarily all countries. By contrast, *global* includes everything on the planet all the way down to the magma. So while an "international" portfolio might have a smattering of non-US investments, a "global" portfolio avails itself to investment options throughout the globe. As such, a true global approach requires a thorough analysis of the composition of global stock markets.

Once you know something about the countries, sectors, and industries that comprise global markets, you can use that information as a guide to building a global portfolio. The approach you take can be either *active* or *passive.*

Definition

Active or Passive

Investors can be either *active* or *passive. Active* investors try to build portfolios that do better than the overall market by choosing investments they think will be better than average. Active investors might concentrate their portfolios in countries, sectors, or individual stocks they expect to outperform the broader market. Of course, things don't always work out the way active investors expect, often causing them to do worse than the market. By contrast, *passive* investors simply try to match the performance of the market. It's often difficult for passive investors to track the market perfectly, but they try to get as close as they can.

The passive approach is relatively easy. You simply construct a portfolio that tracks global markets as closely as possible (less fees, of course) and leave it alone. Go on vacation, take up a hobby. An occasional peek at your account statement and a few adjustments every once in a while are the extent of your required involvement. For the most part, the portfolio takes care of itself. In fact, you may not need to buy a single individual stock! The downside is you're likely to underperform global markets, year in and year out, thanks to fees— but not by much if you do it right.

If the active approach is your cup of tea, you're in for a little more work. Expanding your investment horizons overseas means expanding the number of factors you must consider. But in return, you'll have many more opportunities to add value and manage risk. Both of these strategies will be covered more in depth later in the book.

The Global View

If you expected this book to tell you which countries are going to provide the best returns over the next several years, you're in for a disappointment. The investment world is a dynamic place. By the time this book is written, edited, and hits the bookstore shelves, the environment is likely to have changed. What this book does is give you the tools required to monitor and analyze global economies and markets yourself.

Global investing not only bestows innumerable benefits on your investment portfolio, it just might teach you a thing or two you didn't know about this wide world of ours. The journey is part of the reward, as they say. So read on, enjoy, and tread confidently into the world of global investing so you too can *Own the World*.

Not as Foreign as You Think

Many investors shy away from global investing because they fear the "foreign" part. They think they aren't familiar with foreign companies, economies, or markets. American investors read American newspapers, deposit paychecks at American banks, shop at American supermarkets, watch American movies, eat American foods—it seems like all the things we know and love are produced by America Inc., and that's the way we like it. Occasionally, we might be coerced into sampling some exotic foreign cheese or attending an opera we can't understand, but these sojourns are few and far between. Or so we think. Whether we realize it or not, foreign-made products play significant roles in our everyday lives.

MADE IN THE USA

Every day, we're reminded that some products we use regularly are made here in the US and some aren't. Check the tag of the shirt you're wearing. It'll give you a hint about where it was made. Even if it's an American brand sold by an American firm, chances are it was stitched together in a country where it could be made more cheaply. "Globalization" and its foes have been a hot topic in recent years as more things we use are produced abroad.

Many fear buying foreign-made products means shipping US jobs overseas. This has led, at times, to backlashes by the media and even politicians against free trade. From "Made in the USA" labels (and the Federal Trade Commission stipulating how they can be used) to protectionist legislation emanating from Capitol Hill, "Buy American" is a popular refrain from sea to shining sea.

Why do some people favor American-made products? Maybe they believe the quality is better or the style is more in line with their tastes. (Although those who cheerfully buy foreign goods probably make the same claims.) Maybe foreign-made substitutes simply aren't available. But fearing the loss of American jobs on a broad scale should be far, far down the list.

Actually, it shouldn't make the list at all. Remember Bill Clinton sporting a clever "NAFTA: We HAFTA" baseball cap as he rallied support for the North American Free Trade Agreement? Many— including former presidential contender Ross Perot, who warned of a "giant sucking sound" as jobs left America—feared the trilateral agreement among the US, Canada, and Mexico would result in US manufacturing jobs becoming extinct. But just as folks were too quick to write off the coelacanth and the ivory-billed woodpecker (both were thought to be extinct but were later discovered living), US manufacturing has persevered.

Over a decade later, NAFTA still has its fair share of both proponents and opponents. The latter argue NAFTA has been detrimental to some sectors of the US economy. But it is undeniable that overall employment has been better in the dozen years following NAFTA than it was in the dozen years prior. As of yet, no giant sucking sound has materialized. Figure 2.1, showing imports increasing

Figure 2.1   US Imports and Employment

Source: Thomson Datastream.

while unemployment has generally dropped, proves these fears were unwarranted.

Unemployment fell through the 1990s, rose in the early 2000s, and fell again to near historically low levels. Increased foreign trade isn't to blame for fluctuations in employment today. In fact, many Americans are employed in America by foreign companies that set up shop within our borders.

Outsourcing...to the US?

Why would a foreign firm, domiciled abroad, establish operations in America? After all, we "outsource" some of our own corporate functions to other nations to reduce costs. What's the benefit of having operations here? Foreign companies come to the US for many of the same reasons American firms set up shop overseas. Producing goods close to where they're sold has a variety of benefits, including reduced transportation costs. It can be expensive to transport goods, and the most cost-effective means of transportation are often the slowest.

Sending goods cheaply means it will take longer to get them to markets and generate revenue. So it behooves many firms to produce goods as close as possible to the places they're sold.

Another reason is currency exchange rate fluctuation. Later chapters cover how currencies affect investors, but currencies are arguably even more important for firms doing business abroad. Unless they're specifically trying to profit from currency movements (a goal of some financial firms), most firms would rather eliminate their exposure to fickle exchange rates because they pose risks to profitability. Producing goods in one country and selling them in another exposes a company to currency risk, which could drive costs up and revenues down. For example, if your shirt was made in Thailand, the firm you bought it from pays some of its workers in Thai baht even though it's selling shirts in US dollars. If the value of the baht rises against the dollar, it costs the company more dollars to pay Thai employees. Producing goods in the country they're sold insulates against currency fluctuations because many costs will be in the same currency as sales, making profit margins more stable.

The US consumes more of just about everything than other nations, so it's not surprising many foreign companies have established operations here.

Foreign Firms on Auto Row

The auto industry provides a good example of the role of foreign goods in the US. America's affinity for automobiles has made America the most important market for automobile manufacturers, as evidenced by the breakdown of global vehicle sales illustrated in Figure 2.2.

US drivers buy over 16 million of the 69 million vehicles sold around the world every year—over 23 percent. Increasingly, these vehicles are produced by foreign firms. Non-US firms sell more cars in America than US companies do—although the inclusion of trucks and sport utility vehicles gives US automakers the edge in total vehicle sales.

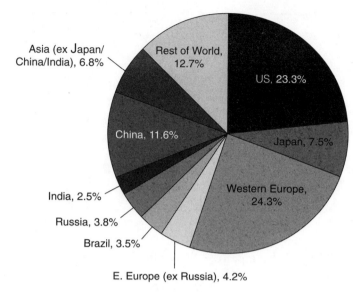

Figure 2.2   2007 Global Vehicle Sales
Source: Goldman Sachs International Research.

Foreign firms are selling more cars in the US, but they're making more of their cars here as well. The Japanese are the most prolific carmakers in the world, building more cars per year than any other country—about 11.5 million in 2007 alone![1] Toyota has surpassed General Motors in total global sales, making it the largest automobile manufacturer by just about any measure (except possibly legacy pension and health-care costs). According to the Japan Automobile Manufacturers Association, almost 70 percent of Japanese cars sold in the US are made here, too. Meanwhile, domestic production by US automakers has been declining. Foreign auto companies are throwing lifelines to a domestic industry that's been faltering for years. Figure 2.3 shows how US production by Japanese automakers has increased over the last 20 years.

All of this translates to foreign companies hiring more US employees. Foreign companies now employ 32 percent of all US auto industry workers—a significant increase over the last 10 years.

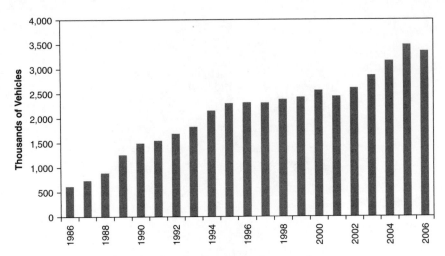

Figure 2.3   US Production by Japanese Automakers
Source: Japan Automobile Manufacturers Association Inc.

Bullit

Just as foreign car companies have been increasing their presence in the US, US auto-makers have been taking advantage of lower production costs in foreign countries. Today, some of the most venerable US automobiles, or at least many of their parts, are produced outside the US. The Ford Mustang is one example. The Mustang first appeared in the 1960s and has been the quintessential American car ever since. Steve McQueen racing a 1968 390 Fastback through the streets of San Francisco in the movie *Bullit* cemented America's love affair with the Mustang. But a significant amount of today's Mustang parts are actually produced abroad. Eyeing lower costs, Ford Motor Company buys many of its parts from foreign suppliers. In fact, it's possible your Toyota contains more American-made components than your Ford! Unpatriotic, you say? We'd argue pioneering ways to produce goods more cheaply and efficiently is as American as Lewis and Clark's expedition to the Pacific.

Source: Jathon Sapsford and Norihiko Shirouzu, "Mom, Apple Pie and…Toyota?" *Wall Street Journal* (May 11, 2006).

Do What You Do Best, America

This book isn't intended to wax philosophic about globalization—there are enough recent books on the topic to fill a library. Some extol the benefits of globalization, while others decry its detriment. Like it or hate it, free trade is the engine that makes globalization go—so understanding the economic impacts of free trade is the cornerstone of understanding the effects of globalization.

Free trade benefits all countries by enabling them to do what they do best (or most efficiently) and buy the rest from others. If you're a great cook but a lousy gardener, and your neighbor has a green thumb but can't toast bread, you both eat better by letting him grow the tomatoes while you cook them. Free trade works the same way. When countries produce the things they make most efficiently and trade with other countries, everybody gets more for their efforts. That's easy to see.

But it's not the overall impact of globalization that makes people fret. It's the inequality of the distribution of the benefits. Workers in some industries are inevitably displaced when their jobs can be performed more cheaply abroad, while workers in other industries benefit from new opportunities. Sneaker assembly-line workers in the US are probably cursing their Air Jordans due to the fact over 90 percent of the shoes we wear in the US are stitched up overseas.[2] But those selling financial services are ecstatic about the opportunities globalization affords financial firms.

The trees undoubtedly block the view of the globalization forest to a certain extent, but the forest is an enchanted one for America.

A DAY IN THE LIFE

Just how foreign are foreign firms? Let's examine a day in the life of an average American.

Rise and Shine

If you're like me, the first thing you do after rolling out of bed is seek out that all-important cup of coffee. Whether it's a latte, cappuccino, mocha, or just a regular cup of joe, the day doesn't really get started until the caffeine kicks in. But without foreign-grown coffee beans, we'd have a tough time peeling ourselves off the mattress. Virtually all the coffee we drink comes from foreign countries.

The main reason is climate. Coffee needs hotter climes than we have in most parts of the US, so it's primarily grown closer to the equator. Hawaii's climate is warm enough to yield great-tasting Kona coffee. But harvesting beans from the volcanic mountain slopes is challenging, so the amount of coffee produced by the 50th state isn't nearly enough to keep the country's heartbeat racing. Without imported coffee, we'd be paying a boatload for those scarce Kona beans.

So we turn to countries like Brazil (the world's largest coffee producer), Mexico, and Guatemala. Foreign beans are often purchased by American coffee companies and put in Folgers cans or Starbucks bags.

Most Important Meal of the Day

Breakfast is next. If yogurt is on the menu, there's a good chance you'll be enjoying a product made by the French company Groupe Danone. Groupe Danone sells more fresh dairy products than any other company in the world. Danone makes Dannon yogurt and holds a controlling stake in Stonyfield Farm, a well-known US dairy producer. Danone produces a number of other commonly used food products, many of which are distributed around the world, including the US.

Rub-a-Dub-Dub, Foreign Products in My Tub

Ready to hit the shower? Unilever, a UK-based firm, makes some of the most popular cleansing products in the US. The Dove brand cleansing bar, a Unilever product, outsells all other cleansing bars in the US combined.[3] In 2007, Unilever sold over €2.5 billion ($3.7 billion) worth of Dove products in over 80 countries.[4] Unilever also makes Vaseline products, the top-selling hand and body lotion in the US.

Running Errands All Over the World

Now that you're awake, fed, and clean, it's time to jump in the car and run a few errands. As mentioned earlier, many of the cars we drive are made by foreign firms. Toyota, BMW, Nissan, Mitsubishi, Mercedes-Benz, Hyundai—there are over 90 different car companies operating around the world. And quite a few of them sell cars here in the US. But it's not just the cars themselves that are made by foreign companies, but also the parts. Tires for instance. Firestone is one of the oldest and best-known tire brands in America. But even though it's got American roots, it's actually a subsidiary of a foreign firm. In 1979, Japan's Bridgestone bought Firestone to form the largest tire company in the world.

Fill 'er Up

If the tank needs filling, it's time for another product from overseas. The majority of the oil consumed in the US is imported. We consume over 20 million barrels of oil per day, and over 60 percent of that comes from elsewhere.[5] Canada, Saudi Arabia, and Mexico are the biggest oil exporters to the US, but we get oil from all parts of the world. Kuwait, Algeria, Chad—even these small countries send oil our way. Foreign firms not only sell us foreign oil, they also help extract oil from US reservoirs, refine oil here in the US, and sell refined products such as gasoline, heating oil, and diesel. BP Plc (formerly called British Petroleum), a company headquartered in the UK, operates our largest oil reservoir—Alaska's Prudhoe Bay oil field. BP also refines gasoline here and sells it through Arco, am/pm, and many independent stations. Similarly, Shell Oil, the US market leader with over 14,000 gas stations operating across the country, is the US affiliate of Netherlands-based Royal Dutch Shell.

Foreign Products on Aisle Nine

Need to pick up some groceries? A trip to the grocery store is about as American as it gets, right? Not necessarily. Depends on where you shop. Three of the 10 largest food distributors in the US are owned by foreign companies.[6] Ahold is an Amsterdam-based company that runs Stop & Shop and Giant Foods supermarkets. Delhaize Group is headquartered in Brussels and owns several grocery store chains including Food Lion, Hannaford, and Sweetbay. The ubiquitous

7-Eleven stores we have turned to for years for Slurpees and other late-night junk food are franchised from Seven & I, a Japanese Company. Incidentally, Seven & I has taken a well-known US brand back home, running Denny's restaurants in Japan.

Do I Get a Free Wok With That Checking Account?

Banking is next on the to-do list. Foreign-run banks also have a significant presence in America. Over 200 foreign banking families have almost 500 branches or subsidiaries here. Combined, they hold over $2.6 trillion in assets.[7] Some of these banks are obviously foreign. It's pretty clear Bank of Tokyo, Unicredito Italiano, and Bayerische Landesbank hail from foreign lands, but others are less obvious. Bank of the West, with $58 billion in assets, is owned by French bank BNP Paribas. Union Bank of California has $52 billion and is owned by Mitsubishi UFJ Financial Group, a Japanese firm. Charter One and Citizens Bank have a combined $115 billion in assets and are owned by Royal Bank of Scotland PLC.[8]

Drink in the Foreign Goodness

All this running around has undoubtedly made you thirsty. By now, you're probably not surprised to read foreign companies sell some of the most popular beverages in the US. The aforementioned Groupe Danone owns the Evian brand and is the second largest peddler of H_2O in the world. Unilever owns Lipton brand tea and sells nearly three times as much Lipton as the closest tea-slinging competitor. Cadbury Schweppes, a UK company, owned 7 Up, Dr. Pepper, Snapple, and Hawaiian Punch drinks before spinning off its US beverage unit in 2008 (incidentally, Cadbury still makes Trident, the world's most popular gum, as well as Dentyne). Even if you're craving something a bit harder than water or soda, American icon Budweiser brand beer is set to go foreign as Belgian beverage company InBev prepares to acquire US brewer Anheuser-Busch.

Fido Likes Foreign, Too

Time to get home and feed the pets. Don't worry, Fido and Mr. Whiskers like foreign treats too. Nestlé, the Swiss company most people associate with chocolate, makes a host of other products, including Purina brand pet foods and products. Alpo, Friskies, Dog Chow, Purina One, Tidy Cats—foreign companies make even our pets' favorites!

Time to Relax in Front of the Tube

It's been a long day. Why not settle down in front of the TV and watch a show? Most of the TVs sold in the US are foreign made. Samsung is a South Korean electronics conglomerate. Sony is a Japanese firm that makes a multitude of widely used consumer products, including PlayStation video game consoles and Bravia televisions. Panasonic televisions are products of Japanese company Panasonic Corporation (formerly Matsushita Electric). Toshiba, Hitachi, and Sharp also call the Land of the Rising Sun home.

Too Much of a Foreign Thing

If your stomach is upset because you sat through *Weekend at Bernie's II* (released by TriStar Pictures, a subsidiary of Columbia pictures, which is owned by Sony Pictures), there's not much any company, foreign or domestic, can do for you. But if your heartburn is the result of too many Raisinets (another Nestlé product), you might think about popping a Tums, made by UK-based pharmaceutical company GlaxoSmithKline, or a Nexium, the product of another UK firm, AstraZeneca.

As you can see, Americans use quite a few foreign products on a daily basis. The products I've mentioned are a very small sample of the many, many goods made by foreign companies that impact our lives here in the US. Table 2.1 includes some of these and other foreign-made products well known to US consumers.

This list is far from exhaustive. And even if a product has a US company's label, there's a good chance some, if not all, of it was produced or

Table 2.1   Taking the Mystery Out of Foreign

Company Name (Country)	US Product Lines
AstraZeneca (UK)	Nexium®—acid reflux-related disease medication
	Seroquel®—bipolar disorder medication
AXA Group (France)	AllianceBernstein
BP Global (UK)	BP fuel (sold to Arco and am/pm)
Credit Suisse (Switzerland)	Parent company of Credit Suisse-First Boston
GlaxoSmithKline	Tums®, NicoDerm®, Nicorette®
Hitachi (Japan)	Hitachi® TVs, VCRs, stereo equipment
ING (Netherlands)	ING Direct online banking service
LVMH Moët Hennessy Louis	Dom Pérignon®, Hennessy Cognac®, TAG Heuer®
Vuitton (France)	DKNY®, Louis Vuitton®, Sephora®
Panasonic Corporation (Japan)	Panasonic®, Quasar®, JVC®
Mitsubishi-Tokyo Financial Group (Japan)	Union Bank of California
Nissan Motors (Japan)	Maxima®, Altima®, Pathfinder®, Infiniti®
Royal Dutch Petroleum (Netherlands)	Shell® gas stations
Sanofi-Aventis (France)	Allegra®—allergy medication
	Ambien®—insomnia medication
Sony Corp. (Japan)	PlaystationTM, TVs, DVD players
	Sony Records®
UBS (Switzerland)	UBS (Formerly Paine Webber)
The Virgin Group (UK)	Virgin Megastore®, Virgin Atlantic Airways®

assembled overseas. For example, semiconductors are key components of anything with electrons flowing through them these days, and some of the largest semiconductor makers are foreign companies. US-based Intel is the biggest, but companies such as Samsung (South Korea) and Taiwan Semiconductor (you guessed it, Taiwan) are also major players in the business. And much of our basic materials are imported. We use copper for everything from construction to penny-pinching, and a large portion of the copper we consume comes from overseas. Same thing with steel and several other important metals. Imports account for the majority of some of the most commonly used resources here in the US.

It's a Two-Way Street

Don't think the presence of foreign products here is a one-way street. These days, US firms generate a significant portion of their revenues overseas. In fact, many of the largest US companies do more business abroad than here. Table 2.2 provides some examples of US companies with significant overseas sales.

According to Standard & Poor's, US firms that break out sales by region report about 44 percent of their revenue in aggregate is generated overseas.[9] For most of these firms, non-US sales are growing much faster than US sales. So it's no wonder US firms are increasingly turning their attention abroad.

Table 2.2   US Companies' Overseas Sales

Company	Percent Foreign Sales (2007)
Qualcomm Inc	86.9%
Intel Corp	84.3%
Transocean Inc	80.3%
Nike Inc	65.8%
McDonald's Corp	65.3%
3M Co	63.3%
Caterpillar Inc	62.0%
Procter & Gamble Co	58.2%
Oracle Corp	57.0%
Adobe Systems Inc	56.3%
Citigroup Inc	54.6%
Chevron Corp	54.2%
United Technologies Corp	51.4%
Goldman Sachs Group Inc	49.1%
Johnson & Johnson	46.9%
Microsoft Corp	40.5%

Source: Bloomberg Finance L.P.

The Global View

Don't fear foreign companies, embrace them. Avoiding investment opportunities overseas means not only avoiding some of the world's best companies, it also means avoiding some of the companies we rely on the most—whether we know it or not.

The prominence of foreign companies in our lives isn't likely to abate anytime soon. Neither is importance of foreign firms in our investment portfolios. Fearing investing in foreign companies doesn't make any more sense than refusing to buy gas for your car just because the oil came from outside the US. Foreign companies and products are here to stay, and that's good for both American consumers and investors.

3

Getting More
for Less

Return Enhancement and Risk
Management

I sincerely hope you read this book cover to cover, but if you only have time for one chapter, this should be the one. This chapter demonstrates the real benefits of global investing. After all, although global investing is easier than ever, some aspects do require more work than domestic-only investing. If you're not getting better results, why put in the effort? You must get more bang for your investment buck, so to speak.

So what is it that makes global investing worthwhile? Quite a bit, actually.

RISK AND RETURN: THE DYNAMIC DUO

Arguably the two most important investing considerations are *risk* and *return*. Risk and return go together like peanut butter and jelly, like lobster and butter, like Batman and Robin (only without the tights). But understanding the relationship between risk and return isn't as straightforward as people frequently think.

Some investors mistakenly believe there's a direct relationship between risk and return. The mantra: The more risk you take, the more return you should ultimately receive. This doctrine isn't wholly wrong. You do have to take some risk to get a decent return. There's no such thing as a risk-free investment. Even stashing cash under your mattress involves risk: burglary, fire, or even bed bugs! And for that, you get no return. In fact, the value of your stashed cash deteriorates over time, if not because of bed bugs, then because of inflation.

Or you could deposit cash in a liquid savings account at an FDIC-insured bank or buy short-term US Treasuries. Both are about as risk-free as you can get. But both offer meager returns, especially when factoring in inflation's impact. Over the last 20 years, the real return (i.e., factoring in inflation) on Treasury Bills has been a paltry 1.5 percent.[1]

Definition

Inflation

Inflation is a term in economics referring to a state of generally rising prices. Most countries measure several different types of inflation. Consumer prices are gauged using a consumer price index (CPI) or some similar measure. Many countries also track producer prices, or the prices paid by most corporations, prices for basic materials, import prices, etc.

Inflation measures usually track the price of a basket of goods and services. So even if prices are generally rising, prices of some things in the basket are undoubtedly rising faster than others. Some prices might even be falling! Often, countries will strip out the most volatile components of inflation to come up with "core" inflation. In the US, core consumer price inflation excludes food and energy prices.

But simply heaping on risk doesn't ensure you'll do much better. Risk and return are intimately intertwined, so getting the best of either requires an understanding of both.

All Categories Are Created Equal

First, a look at return. The return on an investment is simply the amount the value changes over some time period. Stock returns are primarily, but not solely, the result of changes in the market price of the shares. Companies also pay dividends, spin off subsidiaries, issue warrants, or perform other corporate actions that boost or detract from returns—sometimes significantly. You can find returns for a number of stocks and stock indexes in any newspaper's business section or online. Usually, these sources provide *price returns*. You might have to dig a little deeper to find the *total return*.

Don't Forget the Dividend

Often, investors calculating stock or index returns only consider the price change. For many stocks, price changes account for the majority of returns. But it's also important to consider dividends, which add to returns as well.

Considering only changes in prices is known as the *price return*. But if you factor in dividends (and other corporate actions), you're looking at the *total return*. To get a true total return, you must also assume the dividend is reinvested in shares.

The difference between price return and total return can be more significant than you might think. In 2004, after the maximum US tax rate on qualified dividends was reduced to 15 percent, many firms decided to give some cash back to shareholders via dividends. For example, in November 2004, Microsoft paid shareholders a special $3 per share dividend—about 10 percent of the share price. On a price return basis, Microsoft shares lost 2.4 percent in 2004. But Microsoft's total return that year was a much more pleasing +8.9 percent.

Figure 3.1 shows the difference between Microsoft's price return and total return in 2004. Notice the price return dropped off dramatically once Microsoft issued the dividend. Dividends not only boost the total return, but they also subtract from the price return. After all, the company is giving away money! But don't be fooled. What matters most is total return.

Figure 3.1   Microsoft: Price and Total Return in 2004
Source: Thomson Datastream.

As most investors know, certain types of stocks do better than others at times. Sometimes large stocks have better returns than small stocks; bank stocks outdo technology stocks; growth stocks beat value stocks. Look at any major category of stocks—sometimes it does better than other categories, and sometimes it does worse. Returns for foreign and domestic stocks are no exceptions.

Figure 3.2 shows periods in which US stocks have outperformed foreign stocks and vice versa. The graph shows US stock performance (measured by the MSCI USA Index) divided by foreign stock performance (measured by the MSCI EAFE Index). When the line is rising, US stocks are doing better than foreign, and when the line is falling, foreign is outperforming. Sometimes one outperforms the other by a lot, sometimes by a little. And the outperformance periods are very irregular.

The fact foreign stocks sometimes lead domestic stocks and sometimes domestic leads foreign probably isn't surprising. Changes in market leadership make intuitive sense to most investors because we know there are a multitude of differences among countries. Different countries have different economic growth rates, monetary policies,

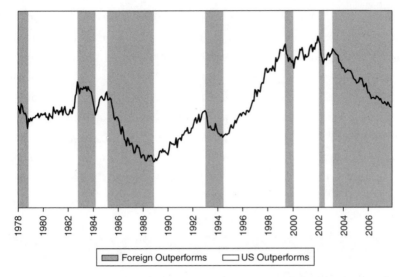

Figure 3.2   Periods of Foreign and Domestic Market Outperformance 1977–2007

Source: Thomson Datastream; MSCI, Inc.[2]

political environments, demographics, alphabets, favorite foods—the list is endless. So in the short term, a host of factors can increase or decrease investors' appetites for stocks all over the world. Chapter 5 covers some of these. For now, the important thing to understand is they influence the *demand* side of the supply-demand equation.

That's right. It's time to break out your Economics 101 textbook.

The Voting Machine

> In the short run, the market is a voting machine, but in the long run, it's a weighing machine.
>
> —Benjamin Graham

You might have heard Benjamin Graham's famous quote and thought he was offering a stock tip about a company producing bathroom scales. But what he was really talking about was *supply* and *demand*.

Stocks are like anything else bought and sold in a free market—their prices are determined by supply and demand. In the short term, demand has the upper hand in determining prices. Why? The supply of many products can be adjusted quickly. Most cars can be assembled in a day. Companies like Dell and Lenovo churn out computers even more quickly. And just about anything electronic can be delivered almost instantaneously via the Internet. But the supply of stocks isn't so malleable. New stocks usually come to market via initial public offerings (IPOs) or secondary offerings, which don't happen overnight.

Definition

Initial Public Offering

Ever wonder where stocks come from? Sadly, there's no stock fairy leaving shares under our pillows as we sleep. Most stocks come to market via *initial public offerings*. When a private company wants to raise money in the stock market, it sells some of its shares to investors and becomes a publicly traded company. This initial share sale is commonly known as an IPO. Some firms might sell more shares down the road, but these are sold via secondary offerings.

It is possible for a company to have more than one IPO. Sometimes, investors such as private equity firms will take public companies private by buying up all their shares. After some time, these companies can be taken public again through another IPO.

At times, it might have seemed like new shares were being introduced daily. And sometimes they were! But investment bankers weren't dreaming up these deals one day and selling shares the next. There's a lot of legal wrangling, number crunching, auditing, and selling that takes place before a share of stock is put on the market. The same is true for corporate mergers, acquisitions, and share repurchases—it takes a relatively long time to effect any of these supply-changing events. And the public gets forewarning well in advance of an impending offering. So in the short term, the stock supply is relatively fixed and demand rules the day.

The Weighing Machine.   However, in the long term, supply takes over. Crafty investment bankers, venture capitalists, and corporate executives can see when a particular category of stocks gets hot and want to participate in the fun by issuing shares there, too! And they don't want to participate in not-so-hot categories, so fewer shares are issued there. Strong demand can keep prices rising, even though new supply is hitting the market. And the higher prices rise, the more supply gets created!

Eventually supply simply outpaces demand. Either there are no more buyers or prices just get too high and interest falls off—and prices fall—sometimes dramatically. Look back no further than the beginning of the millennium to see the magnificent greed at work. In the first quarter of 2000, there was an average of four public stock offerings every trading day in the US alone.[3] Globally, there were over 13 offerings per day!

The exact opposite has been occurring with increasing speed throughout 2005, 2006, 2007, and even into 2008—supply has been shrinking, not growing. New shares are still being issued, but firms have also been repurchasing their shares and using cash to buy other firms at a fervent pace. In 2007 alone, S&P 500 companies bought back almost $600 billion worth of their shares[4]—an all-time record resulting in a meaningful reduction of stock supply.

What does shifting supply mean for investors? It means no stock category will be permanently better or permanently worse than another. The weighing machine won't let it happen. If US stocks outperform foreign stocks for long enough, you can be sure US firms will be selling shares faster than you can say "I-P-O." Eventually, new supply catches up with demand, US stocks start to lag their foreign counterparts, and then the reverse inevitably happens.

In fact, returns for all major categories of stocks are essentially the same over the long term when properly accounted. Don't believe it? Review Figure 3.2 again showing foreign and domestic stock return over the last few decades. For the 30 years from 1977 through 2007, US stocks' average annualized return was a not-too-shabby 11.7 percent.

Over the same period, foreign stocks returned 12.0 percent annualized—a virtual dead heat.[5]

Since 2002, foreign stocks have done better than US stocks, and some pundits give any number of reasons why they think that trend will continue indefinitely. Trade deficits, budget deficits, onerous regulation, obesity, subpar SAT scores, Bob Barker leaving "The Price Is Right"—all cited as causes for the eventual demise of US stocks. On the flip side are investors who steadfastly believe US stocks will always be better long-term investments. Either might be right for a while, but they'll both be wrong in the long run.

Leadership Keeps Changing. By now, you're probably wondering why you wasted your time and money on a book about global investing that tells you returns on stocks outside the US aren't going to be any better than your domestic investments. Don't toss the book in the trash just yet—we're just getting to the good stuff! First of all, returns on foreign stocks can be better than US stocks—much better, in fact. They just won't be permanently better. As you can see in Table 3.1, it's a rare year when US stocks produce either the best or the worst returns. This table shows the performance of the five best-performing and the five worst-performing developed markets over the last 20 years.[6]

So in any given year, investing abroad can make a meaningful difference to your portfolio's returns.

Return's Not-So-Evil Twin

The fact returns even out over the long term makes the second half of our dynamic duo all the more important, so let's turn our attention to *risk*.

When thinking about risk in our everyday lives, we usually contemplate things that can go wrong. Getting behind the wheel of a car involves the risk of getting in an accident. Biting into a slice of pizza too soon can blister the roof of your mouth. Just doing laundry could entail discovering a bright red shirt found its way into the

Table 3.1   Top and Bottom Five Countries

Top Five Countries

1988	Belgium 54%	Denmark 53%	Sweden 48%	Norway 42%	France 38%
1989	Austria 104%	Germany 46%	Norway 46%	Denmark 44%	Singapore 42%
1990	UK 10%	Hong Kong 9%	Austria 6%	Norway 1%	Denmark -1%
1991	Hong Kong 50%	Australia 34%	USA 30%	Singapore 25%	New Zealand 18%
1992	Hong Kong 32%	Switzerland 17%	USA 6%	Singapore 6%	France 3%
1993	Hong Kong 117%	Finland 83%	Singapore 68%	New Zealand 68%	Switzerland 46%
1994	Finland 52%	Norway 24%	Japan 21%	Sweden 18%	Ireland 14%
1995	Switzerland 44%	USA 37%	Sweden 33%	Spain 30%	Netherlands 28%
1996	Spain 40%	Sweden 37%	Portugal 36%	Finland 34%	Hong Kong 33%
1997	Portugal 47%	Switzerland 44%	Italy 35%	Denmark 35%	USA 33%
1998	Finland 122%	Belgium 68%	Italy 53%	Spain 50%	France 42%
1999	Finland 153%	Singapore 99%	Sweden 80%	Japan 62%	Hong Kong 60%
2000	Switzerland 6%	Canada 5%	Denmark 3%	Norway -1%	Italy -1%
2001	New Zealand 8%	Australia 2%	Ireland -3%	Austria -6%	Belgium -11%
2002	New Zealand 24%	Austria 17%	Australia -1%	Norway -7%	Italy -7%
2003	Greece 70%	Sweden 65%	Germany 64%	Spain 58%	Austria 57%
2004	Austria 72%	Norway 53%	Greece 46%	Belgium 44%	Ireland 43%
2005	Canada 28%	Japan 26%	Austria 25%	Denmark 24%	Norway 24%
2006	Spain 49%	Portugal 47%	Ireland 47%	Singapore 47%	Norway 45%
2007	Finland 49%	Hong Kong 41%	Germany 35%	Greece 33%	Norway 31%

Bottom Five Countries

1988	Switzerland 6%	UK 6%	Austria 1%	New Zealand -14%	Portugal -29%
1989	Spain 10%	Australia 9%	Hong Kong 8%	Japan 2%	Finland -10%
1990	Sweden -21%	Portugal -31%	Finland -32%	Japan -36%	New Zealand -38%
1991	Italy -2%	Portugal -5%	Austria -12%	Norway -15%	Finland -18%
1992	Japan -21%	Spain -22%	Italy -22%	Norway -22%	Denmark -28%
1993	UK 24%	Belgium 24%	France 21%	Canada 18%	USA 9%
1994	Canada -3%	Spain -5%	France -5%	Austria -6%	Hong Kong -29%
1995	Finland 5%	Italy 1%	Japan 1%	Portugal 0%	Austria -5%
1996	Belgium 12%	Austria 5%	Switzerland 2%	Singapore -7%	Japan -16%
1997	Australia -10%	New Zealand -14%	Hong Kong -23%	Japan -24%	Singapore -30%
1998	Hong Kong -3%	Canada -6%	Singapore -13%	New Zealand -23%	Norway -30%
1999	Switzerland -7%	Portugal -9%	Austria -9%	Ireland -13%	Belgium -14%
2000	Belgium -17%	Sweden -21%	Singapore -28%	Japan -28%	New Zealand -34%
2001	Singapore -23%	Italy -27%	Sweden -27%	Japan -29%	Finland -38%
2002	Greece -25%	Ireland -26%	Finland -30%	Sweden -30%	Germany -33%
2003	Switzerland 34%	UK 32%	USA 28%	Netherlands 28%	Finland 19%
2004	Japan 16%	Switzerland 15%	Netherlands 12%	USA 10%	Finland 6%
2005	Spain 4%	Italy 2%	New Zealand 2%	Portugal -2%	Ireland -2%
2006	Switzerland 27%	Canada 18%	New Zealand 17%	USA 15%	Japan 6%
2007	Austria 2%	Sweden 1%	Belgium -3%	Japan -4%	Ireland -20%

Source: Thomson Datastream.

whites, turning the entire load pink. Generally, we think of risk as a bad thing.

But investing isn't that simple. Measuring investment risk means measuring the variability of returns, or *volatility*.

Definition

Volatility

Many things can be volatile. We often hear about volatile chemicals. Or we're told so-and-so has a volatile personality. Stocks are volatile, too. Stock *volatility* refers to the amount stock prices move. Stocks with wildly swinging prices are said to be more volatile, while stocks with more subdued prices are less volatile. Some stocks are more volatile than others by virtue of the businesses they're in. For instance, health care, utility, and consumer staples companies tend to be less volatile than stocks in other sectors because their earnings tend to be fairly stable, although this isn't always the case. And the volatility in some stocks rises for stock-specific issues such as corporate mergers or changes in management, which can cause stock prices to jump or fall.

But volatility itself can be volatile. The most stable stocks can seem downright mercurial at times, and the erratic ones can seem calm. This extends to the overall market as well. The volatility in US stocks (measured by the Chicago Board Options Exchange Volatility Index) was at record lows as 2007 began only to spike to phenomenal highs in 2008.

The greater the volatility, the riskier the investment, no matter which direction the investment is going. A stock that increases wildly in value is considered just as "risky" as a stock that drops dramatically because the deviation from expected returns is just as great. Most investors don't see it that way. If a stock jumps up a lot, they're more likely to pat themselves on the back and celebrate their investing success than rationally assess the risk they took. Only when stocks fall do they see the risk involved. Obviously, whether a stock is rising or falling makes a big difference to investors, but volatility is the key measure to consider in portfolio construction.

Rip Van Winkle Never Bothered Grocery Shopping.   Unless you have narcoleptic tendencies rivaling Rip Van Winkle, you should care about investment risk. If you invested your money then dozed off for a few decades, what happened to your portfolio while you were slumbering wouldn't matter much as long as returns were good. (And if you had a reasonably diversified stock portfolio, odds are they probably were!) Fortunately, we're more insomnious than Mr. Van Winkle, so the path our investments take matters. Naturally, we want the straightest path possible. In investing, you should either aim to maximize the return you receive for a given level of risk or target a specific return and minimize the risk taken to achieve it.

Let's cast the financial jargon aside for a moment and draw a comparison to an everyday activity—grocery shopping. Think of the groceries you buy as return and the cost of buying them as risks. When shopping for groceries, you want to get as many groceries as you can for the amount of money you have to spend. Or, if you only need a few specific items, you want to pay as little as possible for them.

At the grocery store, it's easy to tell how much you pay for an item. You look at a price tag or scan a bar code. Unfortunately, stocks don't come with bar codes telling you how risky they will be, but that doesn't mean we can't measure risk. The most common metric used to measure investment risk is *standard deviation*.

Definition

Standard Deviation

Standard deviation is a statistical measure of volatility. It's a calculation of the dispersion of a stock's returns around the average. Essentially, it tells you how much the value of an investment bounces around.

In investing, we use standard deviation to measure risk. By definition, risky stocks have high standard deviations, and less risky stocks have low standard deviations. That doesn't mean one is necessarily going to be better than the other going forward. It means returns on risky stocks are more likely to veer from what you expect than less risky stocks.

Generally, stocks tend to be more volatile than bonds, but, as covered in Chapter 1, you get something in return for bearing that risk—better long-term returns. So thinking of return as good and risk as bad oversimplifies the relationship because it ignores the necessity of risk to achieve returns. You need to pay something for your groceries; that's just the way it goes.

As you might imagine, there's a big difference between a bag of groceries and a portfolio of stocks—a distinction far more important than paper versus plastic. There's a fundamental difference in the way you add up the costs of each. To figure out how much your groceries cost, all you do is add the costs of all the items in your bag. If milk costs three dollars, eggs cost two dollars, and the celebrity gossip magazine you grab as an impulse buy costs one dollar, your total bill comes to six bucks.

But what if adding tomatoes to your bag made the whole bag cost less? In effect, that's how blending different kinds of stocks works. You can actually reduce the risk you "pay" for your return by adding different stocks. What sort of alchemy enables stocks to confer such wondrous benefits on a portfolio?

Zigging and Zagging to Investing Success. Like most *Dancing With the Stars* contestants, stock prices aren't perfectly in sync. In any given day, week, month, or year, some stocks are moving up while others are moving down. And even stocks moving in the same direction do so in different magnitudes. The relationships between the movements of different stocks are known as their *correlations*.

Definition

Correlation Coefficient

One of the most commonly used measures of the relationships between stocks is their *correlation coefficient*. Correlation coefficients always fall into a range of $+1$ to -1. A correlation of $+1$ means the stocks are perfectly correlated—they always move in the same direction. A correlation of -1 means the stocks are perfectly negatively correlated—they always move in opposite directions. A correlation close to zero means the movement of one stock doesn't tell you anything about the other.

In reality, no two stocks are perfectly positively or negatively correlated because all stocks have some things in common, but none have everything in common. That begs the question: What causes these varying degrees of correlation?

Finding an Imperfect Match.   Some companies are very similar. Two potato chip firms of similar size making similar chips of similar quality are going to react similarly to a number of conditions. A busy picnic season could cause demand for their products to surge, benefiting both. A spike in the cost of potatoes could squeeze both their margins. These similarities will likely contribute to a strong correlation between their stock prices.

There will be some company-specific factors preventing them from being perfectly correlated. One firm might make a successful venture into pretzel production. A breakthrough in ruffle technology could give one an edge over the other. Or one could be charged with stealing a nacho-flavoring recipe and face steep legal costs. But for the most part, these companies' stocks should act a lot alike.

By contrast, many firms have very little in common, causing their stock prices to have low or negative correlations. An increase in the demand for potato chips won't much benefit a steel firm, so there's no reason their stock prices should move in lockstep. That doesn't mean returns on potato chip stocks and steel stocks have to be materially different. They might end up with identical returns, but they'll follow different paths to get there.

Herein lays the glorious wonderment of *diversification*. When stocks travel different paths to get to about the same place, you can combine them in a portfolio to reduce risk. That's right—you pay less for your groceries! And you don't have to clip coupons or hunt down a bunch of negatively correlated stocks either. Combining any stocks with less-than-perfect correlations can give you some benefit. But the lower the correlation, the less your groceries cost.

A simple example. Transocean Inc. and BJ Services Co. are both US firms involved in oil and natural gas exploration and production. Big oil firms hire Transocean to drill their offshore oil and gas wells. BJ Services provides various services to drilling firms like Transocean. Their busi-nesses aren't identical, but both companies stand to benefit from factors such as higher oil prices, increased capital spending in the oil and gas industry, and favorable tax treatment for petroleum-related companies. With so much in common, it comes as no surprise their stock prices are highly correlated. Over the last 10 years, their correlation coefficient has been a whopping 0.75.[7] That's not perfect, but it's darn high. And their returns have been almost identical. Transocean's average annual return was 11.0 percent compared to 10.7 percent for BJ Services.[8]

Both stocks tend to jump around a lot, too. The annualized stand-ard deviations of their returns are 45.2 percent for Transocean and 48.0 percent for BJ Services[9]—both well above average for US stocks. So here, we've got two fairly volatile, highly correlated oil stocks with similar returns.

Now imagine 10 years ago, you divided your investment dol-lars equally between these two stocks instead of investing in just one. It turns out that would have been a splendid idea. Your return would simply be the weighted average return of the two stocks, or 10.8 percent annualized. That's virtually identical to the return you would have received had you bought either of the stocks individu-ally. But here's the good part: The volatility of the portfolio falls to

43.7 percent—*lower* than that of either of the individual stocks.[10] This might seem like a small benefit, but it's a benefit nonetheless. And remember—these stocks are highly correlated.

Now let's take a look at what would happen if you added a stock with a lower correlation. Transocean and BJ Services have much in common, but they have almost nothing in common with a company like Cisco Systems, Inc. Cisco is a technology company that makes networking equipment. No offense to the folks at Cisco, but most probably couldn't tell a deepwater drill ship from a tug boat. Their business is affected by different factors entirely. As such, Cisco's stock price and those of our oil companies have low correlations—around 0.25.[11] But Cisco's stock has returned 11.3 percent over the same 10-year period, in line with the others. And Cisco shares are just about as bouncy, with an annual standard deviation of 43.2 percent.[12]

Had you sunk a third of your money in each of these three stocks, you'd barely notice the difference in terms of performance—the portfolio would have returned 11.0 percent annually. But the volatility would have dropped all the way to 34.2 percent![13] Same return—lower risk! Figure 3.3 illustrates this risk-reduction by showing the performance of each of these three volatile stocks and the combined portfolio over the last 10 years.

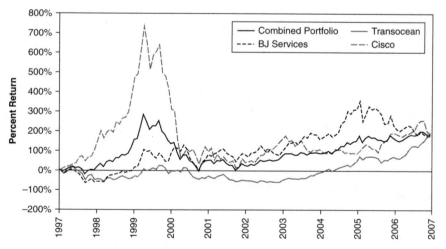

Figure 3.3   Transocean, BJ Services, and Cisco Portfolio 1997–2007
Source: Thomson Datastream.

Leave the Eye of Newt at Home.   This isn't investing voodoo or witchcraft. It's simple math.

In statistics parlance, returns are *linear*, but risks are *non-linear*. Seem obscure and even metaphysical? It's not. More simply—you can add returns together, but you can't add risks. Any individual stock impacts portfolio performance in direct proportion to its weight in the portfolio.

To calculate portfolio return over some time period, you simply calculate the *weighted average return* of all the stocks in the portfolio. This means multiplying each stock's return by the stock's weight in the portfolio to determine the impact of each stock on the portfolio's return. Then you sum the impacts of all the stocks to calculate the return of the entire portfolio. It's as easy as that.

If you had a crystal ball and knew a particular stock's return was going to exceed your portfolio's average return over some period, you could add that stock to boost your portfolio.

Calculating Weighted Average Return

Calculating a weighted average return is really quite simple. Imagine you have a four-stock portfolio of $100,000, in these amounts:

- Stock A—$15,000 (15% of the portfolio)
- Stock B—$20,000 (20% of the portfolio)
- Stock C—$25,000 (25% of the portfolio)
- Stock D—$40,000 (40% of the portfolio).

Over a year, each stock rises a different amount:

- Stock A rises 60%
- Stock B rises 20%
- Stock C rises 35%
- Stock D rises 5%

You can't just add those percentages and divide by four. The smallest stock, A, rose the most, but it had the smallest weight and therefore the smallest impact. The same in reverse for D, the largest stock. To get the correct, weighted average, you simply multiply each stock's return by its weight in the portfolio, and add them together to get the return of the entire portfolio. For example:

$$(15\% * 60\%) + (20\% * 20\%) + (25\% * 35\%) + (40\% * 5\%) = 23.75\%$$

Your portfolio overall rose 23.75 percent! That's the weighted average return.

But risk doesn't work the same way. Imperfect correlations among stocks ensure the risk associated with a multi-stock portfolio will be lower than the weighted average risk of the individual components. For example, in the Transocean-BJ Services-Cisco portfolio, the weighted average standard deviation is 45.5 percent ([1/3 * 48.0%] + [1/3 * 45.25%] + [1/3 * 43.7%] = 45.5%). Compare that to the *actual* standard deviation—34.2 percent. This difference tells you something important: It's how much risk-reducing benefit you're receiving from diversification.

But you can't diversify away all portfolio risk. All stocks have some things in common. There are market-moving events that impact all stocks, no matter their businesses.

A Case of the Mondays.   Take Black Monday for example. On October 19, 1987, the S&P 500 fell over 20 percent in a single day. But losses weren't confined to US stocks. Markets around the world fell dramatically. Stocks lost more value on that day than any other before it. Investors didn't spare banks stocks because they thought the interest rate environment looked favorable. They didn't give shoe companies a break because demand for sneakers was promising. Pretty much every stock in the S&P 500 fell. However, the magnitude of the declines varied quite a bit. Some stocks fell only slightly while others dropped precipitously. But they all ended in negative territory. The risk you can't diversify away is known as *market* or *systemic* risk. Like it or not, that's the risk you must take to get the stock market's superior long-term returns.

KEEP YOUR EYE ON THE GLOBE

And how does this all tie in to global investing? Few events affect stock prices as universally as Black Monday. More common events, like elections and tax code changes, tend to be country-specific or, at most, regional. It takes a real doozy to have global implications.

That's not to say some trends aren't global. From 2003 through 2007, economic growth was strong around the world, thanks largely to the effects of globalization, and stocks in most countries have benefited. Before that, the nasty bear market lasting from 2000 to 2002 weighed on stocks in most countries, save a select few such as Australia, Austria, and New Zealand, which posted flat to positive returns for US investors. And more recently in 2008, a panic among investors globally has caused stocks to plummet everywhere.

But because the environment for stocks differs from country to country, US stocks will tend to have imperfect correlations with foreign stocks. That means global investing opens the door to a treasure trove of risk-reducing opportunities. This is demonstrated in Table 3.2, which lists different countries and their stock markets' average annual return, standard deviation, and correlation to the US stock market over the last 30 years. On the last line is the same information for the world.

Notice US standard deviation has been lower than most. The US economy and stock market are big and diverse enough that a lot of zigging and zagging go on within our borders. But bigger doesn't always mean lower volatility. Japan and the UK, homes of the second and third biggest economies and stock markets, have both been reasonably volatile.

Some argue an increasingly intertwined global economy means stocks in most developed countries will rise and fall together, reducing the benefits of global diversification. But even though these countries have become increasingly correlated in recent years, there's still enough of a difference to make diversification more than worthwhile.

And correlations change over time, so just because they've been more highly correlated recently doesn't mean they will be in the future.

The King of Global Portfolios

The last line of Table 3.2 shows the annualized return, standard deviation, and US correlation for the MSCI World Index, which tracks stocks in developed countries around the world—23 in all—including all those listed in the table. (Believe it or not, some global stock indexes are even more geographically diverse. You'll read more on these later, but the MSCI World Index will do fine for now.)

Table 3.2   Country Returns, Correlations, and Standard Deviations 1977–2007

Country	Annualized Return	Standard Deviation	Correlation to US
US	11.7%	14.7%	1.00
UK	13.3%	18.0%	0.59
Japan	9.1%	22.4%	0.29
France	14.3%	21.8%	0.52
Germany	11.6%	21.5%	0.49
Canada	12.3%	19.2%	0.72
Switzerland	12.3%	17.7%	0.50
Australia	12.9%	22.5%	0.48
Spain	14.3%	22.2%	0.44
Italy	13.5%	24.5%	0.32
Netherlands	14.7%	17.6%	0.63
Hong Kong	16.5%	30.9%	0.39
Sweden	17.1%	24.1%	0.53
Belgium	13.8%	19.3%	0.45
Singapore	11.8%	26.2%	0.50
Norway	14.7%	25.7%	0.49
Denmark	14.3%	18.4%	0.42
Austria	11.4%	21.9%	0.20
World	**11.9%**	**13.9%**	**0.84**

Source: Thomson Datastream, MSCI, Inc.[14]

You'll notice the standard deviation of the MSCI World Index over the last 30 years is lower than that of any of the individual countries, yet the returns are about the same. Sure, a few countries have done better. Take Sweden for example. Sweden's 17.1 percent average annual return over the last 30 years is impressive, but it came at a cost. Swedish stocks were considerably more volatile than a global portfolio. The same is true of Hong Kong. Stocks there did better than a global portfolio, but again, investors shouldered considerable risk to get those returns.

Before you throw caution to the wind and accept the added risk, consider the poor souls who leaned heavily on Japan and Singapore over the last three decades. What did they get for the risk they took? More volatility and worse returns. A global portfolio mitigates the risk associated with any single country, gives you the most opportunity for diversification, and offers the best combination of risk and return.

Currency: Global Investing's Forgotten Stepchild

Earlier, I mentioned dividend yields and changes in prices account for most of you returns. That statement should have come with an asterisk because though it's true for domestic stocks, there's another force at work in a global portfolio that can be just as powerful.

Quite frequently, changes in currency exchange rates have as big an impact on foreign investments as changes in stock prices, at least in the short term. As currencies fluctuate, so do the values of foreign investments when you convert them back to your home currency. This is true for investors in the US, Spain, New Zealand, Austria, Canada—no matter where you hang your hat, changing exchange rates play a large role. The impact of currencies is so important, I've dedicated an entire chapter to the subject (Chapter 8 if you want to peek ahead), but I'd be remiss if I didn't at least mention the effects of exchange rates in a discussion of diversification.

Exchange rates exist between all currencies. At any time, you can figure out how many Japanese yen it takes to buy a Swiss franc or how many euros it takes to buy a Loonie (aka Canadian dollar). But for US investors, US dollar exchange rates matter most.

It works like this: If a US investor buys a stock in the UK that's trading at £100, and the exchange rate between the US dollar and the UK pound is $1.50 ($1.50 buys you £1), the US investor will pay $150 for that share of stock (excluding taxes, fees, etc.). Now imagine the stock price doesn't budge, but the exchange rate slides to $2 per pound. Even if the investor sells the stock exactly where he bought it, he'll make 33% on his investment. Why? Because when he converts the £100 back to US dollars, he'll receive $200. So a falling US dollar actually boosts returns on foreign investments for a US investor. But it's not a one-way street—exchange rates can sap foreign investment returns when the dollar is rising. Currency fluctuations probably won't add or subtract too much from your returns long term (more on this in Chapter 8). But in the short term, currencies can make a big difference.

Rising and falling currencies are continuously increasing and decreasing foreign investment returns. But most exchange rates have virtually nothing to do with stock prices. In other words, there's little if any long-term correlation between currencies and stocks. Table 3.3

**Table 3.3   Correlations Between Exchange
Rates and Stock Prices 1977–2007**

Country	Correlation
Japan	−0.05
France	−0.25
Germany	−0.11
Canada	0.20
Switzerland	−0.25
Spain	−0.05
Netherlands	−0.07
Hong Kong	0.06
Sweden	−0.12
Belgium	−0.11
Norway	−0.24
Denmark	−0.15
Austria	−0.06

Source: Thomson Datastream, Bloomberg Finance L.P.

shows correlations between countries' exchange rates with the US dollar and that country's stock market in its home currency.

These correlations, both positive and negative, are low enough to be just about meaningless. Low to negative long-term correlations and little impact on long-term performance—if you're thinking currency fluctuations might reduce the risk in your portfolio, you're absolutely right! Fluctuating exchange rates enhance the zigging and zagging characteristics of foreign investments, helping increase diversification and reduce risk overall.

The Multinational Myth

As mentioned in Chapter 2, US firms do a lot of business overseas these days. In fact, you'd be hard pressed to find many major US firms that don't have significant overseas sales, operations, or assets. Expanding outside the US benefits firms in a number of ways. It vastly expands the marketplace for their goods and services. It provides access to less expensive and differently skilled employees. Firms often receive more favorable tax treatment outside the US. Doing business overseas can also make it more feasible for a firm to tap foreign financial markets.

But one thing international expansion doesn't do is make US stocks act like foreign stocks. No matter where a firm does business, its shares will be subject to factors impacting stock prices in its home country. Just as there's an overall "market risk" associated with stock investing, there's also "country risk" associated with every nation. Try as you might, this is one risk that can't be diversified away without adding the non-correlated benefits of foreign investments. Country risk in some countries will be more substantial than others, but it exists everywhere.

In most countries, including the US, the largest firms are some of the most internationally active. Since these stocks make up the majority of a country's stock market, it's only natural they act like their home country, not the countries in which they do business. The Morgan Stanley Multinational Index, also known by the catchy name "the New Nifty Fifty," tracks 50 US stocks with significant overseas sales. Figure 3.4 shows the performance of the

Figure 3.4   Multinationals vs. S&P 500 1984–2007
Source: Bloomberg Finance L.P.

New Nifty Fifty compared to the S&P 500 since the multinational index was introduced in 1984.

The multinational index tracks US stocks almost perfectly. The New Nifty Fifty and the S&P 500 have a correlation of over 0.96—these stocks are essentially identical to the broader US market. But its correlation to the MSCI EAFE Index is much lower at 0.55. You get almost zero foreign investing benefit from investing in US multinationals.

The Global View

So there you have it: The benefits of global diversification in one tidy chapter. Keep in mind, looking at historical risk and return won't tell you exactly what the future holds, but they don't have to. Returns, standard deviations, and correlations change over time. At some times, foreign stock markets will be more highly correlated with US stocks than others. As a result, the diversification benefits you receive from global investing won't be constant. But stock markets globally have never been perfectly correlated and they never will be. And there will always be innumerable investment opportunities overseas. Therefore, the benefits of global diversification will persist indefinitely.

The Global
Landscape

To build a global portfolio, you must know what the world looks like. You're undoubtedly aware the earth is round and about two-thirds covered by water. You can probably pick out the seven continents and the various oceans. You might even know the world's highest point is Mount Everest at over 29,000 feet above the sea, and its lowest is the Mariana Trench, two-and-a-half leagues below. This knowledge is infinitely useful for geographers, cartographers, mountain climbers, deep sea divers, and spelunkers. But it's of little use when investing. From an investment standpoint, knowing the global landscape means knowing the relative sizes and compositions of economies and capital markets.

AN ECONOMIC PERSPECTIVE

The days of looking at the world as a loose conglomeration of individual economies are long gone. Globalization has fused once-disparate economies into one vast global economy. As pointed out in Chapter 2, our day-to-day lives wouldn't hum along quite so serenely without foreign products. But even though economies are intertwined as never before, countries retain unique economic characteristics. As you'll read in Chapter 5, economic conditions are extremely important to consider when deciding where to invest. But by and large, we're all swimming in the same economic pool.

Economies and capital markets are inextricably linked. After all, the economy is the engine that makes capital markets go. Without all those nifty components of economic output there wouldn't be much need for companies, governments, or anyone else to raise capital by issuing securities.

The Big Kahuna of Economic Statistics

Month after month, quarter after quarter, and year after year, countries calculate thousands of economic statistics. Consumer prices, producer prices, housing starts, jobless claims, industrial production—the list goes on and on. Some are meaningful for investors, some aren't. But when it comes down to it, the granddaddy of them all is *gross domestic product* (GDP).

Definition

Gross Domestic Product

Gross domestic product (aka GDP) is the total value of all the goods and services produced within a country. Most countries release GDP statistics quarterly, although some do it monthly. In the US, we take the quarter-over-quarter change in GDP and turn that into an annualized number. So if one quarter's GDP increases 1.0% from the previous quarter, GDP is said to have grown at an annualized pace of 4.1% (notice it's not 4.0% since it's a compound annual rate). Some countries focus on just quarter-over-quarter GDP growth without annualizing the data. And others use year-over-year changes in GDP. No matter how you slice it, GDP is intended to measure the same thing just about everywhere.

There are a number of ways to measure an economy's size, but GDP is by far the most common. GDP includes the total value of all goods and services produced in a country's borders. Add the value of every toaster, tractor, movie, car wash—everything you can imagine—produced over a set period, and voilà—you've got GDP.

The GDP calculation includes only finished goods to avoid double counting. If a farmer sells cotton to a textile company, and the textile company sells fabric to a tailor, who turns it into a suit, only the suit counts toward GDP since it should theoretically include the value of all the materials and labor along the way. Even so, figuring out the value of everything a country produces is no small task. Fortunately, economists have come up with a fairly simple equation that aims to do just that.

The ABCs of GDP

Like $E = mc^2$, the simplicity of the GDP equation belies the magnitude of what it accomplishes. This simple equation requiring nothing more than basic addition gives you the economic output for an entire country. The GDP equation is:

$$C + I + G + (X - M) = GDP$$

This equation is used in the expenditure approach to calculating GDP because it sums everything a country buys. You could come up with the same number by measuring the output of each sector of the economy directly. Or you could sum the incomes of people and companies resulting from the production of goods and services. In theory, all three approaches should yield the same result. But the expenditure approach is most commonly used.

So what goes into the GDP equation? Here's a look at the individual components.

- **C** *is for consumption.* Private consumption—it's the stuff we spend money on. By buying this book, you added 0.000000001 percent to US GDP. Go America! Consumption is the largest component of US GDP, just as it is in many countries. Here, it accounts for about 70 percent of the total.

- **I** *is for investment.* Specifically business investment. Not in stocks or bonds or other investments intended to provide some rate of return in the traditional investment sense. Investment in the GDP equation refers to the purchase of things like factory equipment or software—the stuff firms buy to keep their businesses running. But it doesn't factor in depreciation. So it's really "gross investment" rather than "net investment." It also puts the "gross" in gross domestic product.

- **G** *is for government spending.* In case you weren't aware, the government loves spending money. Not just the federal government. States, counties, cities, townships, boroughs—they all spend enthusiastically. All the dough governments receive in taxes gets spent ... and then some.

- **(X − M)** *is for net exports.* Here we're talking net exports, not gross exports. These are the things we sell to other countries minus the things we import. As you probably deduced, *X* is the export part of the equation and *M* is the import part. In the US, we've been importing more than we export continuously for 30 years, meaning we buy more goods and services from other countries than we sell to them.[1] As a result, net exports subtracts from our GDP.

The GDP calculation might seem elementary, but determining accurate inputs isn't. Governments have a hard enough time keeping track of their own expenses, let alone everyone else's. But that doesn't stop them from trying. The data aren't perfect, but at least you don't have to go through the hassle of collecting it yourself. As imperfect as it might be, government GDP calculations are among the best we've got.

GDP's Not All It's Cracked Up to Be

GDP is one of the most widely followed economic statistics. But like virtually all government statistics, it's not without faults. To calculate GDP, governments compile data from many different sources. As you can imagine, it's not easy to account for the value of every single good and service a country produces. Some items are bound to fall through the cracks.

To gather data, governments rely heavily on surveys, especially in the initial report. There are some inherent problems with using survey data. Surveys sample a small group and extrapolate the results to represent a much larger group. It's impossible to get truly accurate results using this approach. That's why survey results always include some margin of error.

Governments also rely on other organizations for much of the data included in the GDP calculations. These data usually aren't collected for the sole purpose of calculating GDP, so the government might have to tweak them to meet its needs.

These inaccuracies necessitate multiple GDP revisions. As mentioned, US GDP is calculated quarterly. The first GDP estimate is released near the end of the month following the quarter's end. The data are then revised the following month and again the month after.

Quarterly GDP data are combined for an annual number. These numbers are then revised each July until a comprehensive revision is conducted about every fifth year. This makes GDP data a bit stale by the time it's truly accurate. For investors, five-year-old data is about as useful as five-day-old sushi.

Get Real . . . or Nominal

If you think you've got GDP figured out, you might have another think coming. Just calculating GDP is one thing, but you also need to decide what kind of GDP you're calculating—*real* or *nominal*.

Definition

Real versus Nominal

Many figures can be calculated in either real or nominal terms. Investment returns, interest rates, economic growth, and many other measures can be real or nominal. *Real* figures strip out the impact of inflation whereas *nominal* figures don't. If the nominal interest rate on a bond is 5 percent and inflation is at 3 percent per year, the "real" interest rate on the bond is 2 percent. If the nominal return on a stock is 10 percent in a given year in the same inflation environment, the real return is 7 percent.

When given the choice between nominal and real GDP, you're probably inclined to go with the latter. Is nominal GDP fake? Is it the *I Can't Believe It's Not Butter* of economic indicators? The difference between real and nominal GDP has nothing to do with trans fats or partially hydrogenated oils. *Nominal* GDP measures the value of everything a country produces using current prices, while *real* GDP uses constant prices. To calculate nominal GDP using the GDP equation, you simply plug in current prices of all the aforementioned expenditures. This is a good measure of the current size of a country's economy, but it's not so useful when measuring how fast an economy is growing. The problem stems from inflation.

Changes to nominal GDP reflect not only economic growth but also rising prices. If a country's economy is growing slowly but inflation is rampant, nominal GDP would show a big jump even though real output might be stagnant. Nominal GDP growth of 20 percent in a year might seem extraordinary, but it's not much to get excited about if inflation is 19 percent.

By contrast, *real* GDP adjusts for inflation, so it's a better measure of economic growth. Since prices tend to rise most of the time in most countries, nominal GDP usually grows faster than real GDP. The opposite is true if prices are falling—a condition known as *deflation*—but that's less common.

The Land of the Rising Sun ... and Falling Prices

Inflation is a common concern for most countries. In fact, many central banks exist primarily to ensure price stability, which usually means fighting inflation. But falling prices can be just as problematic.

Not long ago, the world's second largest economy faced this scenario. After years of booming economic growth and skyrocketing asset prices, Japan's economy cooled and prices began falling. By the late 1990s, Japan's economy was mired in a deflationary spiral that lasted a decade. Take a look at Table 4.1—nominal GDP growth exceeded real GDP growth in 2007 in every country listed except Japan. That's because prices were falling in Japan while they were rising elsewhere.

Falling prices might seem like a dream come true for consumers, but deflation isn't as dreamy as you might think. In fact, deflation causes a number of problems, including an incentive to delay purchases. Why buy that television or stereo today if you can buy it for less in six months? Since fewer purchases mean less economic growth, countries want to keep their cash registers ka-chinging. So Japan's central bank, the Bank of Japan (BOJ), instituted some extreme measures to pump up prices. In a policy known as *quantitative easing*, the BOJ took interest rates down to zero and flooded the banking system with money. The BOJ hoped all this readily available cash would boost prices and do the same for the economy. It's taken awhile, but at long last, it appears Japan is on the verge of defeating deflation.

Table 4.1 shows economic growth rates for a number of different countries. Column two shows the nominal figure. Column three shows real growth. And the fourth column shows the rate of inflation that led to the difference between the two.

Table 4.1   2007 GDP Growth

Country	Nominal GDP Growth	Real GDP Growth	Inflation
US	4.9%	2.2%	2.7%
Japan	1.3%	2.1%	−0.8%
Germany	4.4%	2.5%	1.8%
China	17.0%	11.4%	5.0%
UK	6.3%	3.1%	3.0%
France	4.1%	1.9%	2.2%
Italy	3.8%	1.5%	2.3%
Spain	7.0%	3.8%	3.1%
Canada	5.9%	2.7%	3.1%
Brazil	9.7%	5.4%	4.0%
Russia	22.7%	8.1%	13.5%
India	14.4%	9.2%	4.7%
Australia	8.0%	3.9%	3.9%
Mexico	6.6%	3.3%	3.2%
Netherlands	5.0%	3.5%	1.5%
Turkey	13.3%	5.0%	7.9%
Sweden	6.0%	2.6%	3.3%
Belgium	4.4%	2.7%	1.7%
Indonesia	18.5%	6.3%	11.5%

Source: International Monetary Fund.

WHAT'S YOUR GDP WORTH?

As you'd expect, countries usually calculate their GDP in their home currencies. We calculate our economic output in US dollars. Russians use rubles. Japanese use yen. And most countries in the European Union use euros. How can you compare economies when they're measured in different units? Quite simply, you can't. You need to convert these calculations to a common measure. That basically leaves you with two options. You can use *exchange rates* to convert everything into one common currency. Or you can use a measure known as *purchasing power parity* (PPP).

Definition

Purchasing Power Parity (PPP)

Purchasing power parity is the idea that identical or nearly identical products and services should cost the same no matter where they're sold. If they don't, consumers will favor products in the cheaper country and exchange rates will eventually eliminate the difference in prices. An example: Imagine a television costs €600 in France. If the exchange rate between the US dollar and the euro is $1.50 per euro, that TV costs $900. If consumers can buy the same TV in the US for $500, they'll prefer to buy it here. Eventually, enough consumers trading their euros for dollars will drive the value of the dollar up and the euro down until the TV costs the same in both places. Obviously, price differences on a single product aren't enough to move currency markets, but the purchasing power parity theory assumes price difference on a broad scale will eventually be arbitraged away.

It's important to note purchasing power parity is a theory. And as explained later in this chapter, it's got some glaring holes. But purchasing power parity is one method of gauging the relative values of currencies.

Try Exchange Rates

Using exchange rates to compare GDP is fairly easy. You take the GDP reported in a country's local currency and convert it to a common currency. It doesn't matter which currency you choose as your base. The proportions will all turn out the same. Since we're in the

US, we tend to convert everything to US dollars. For example, Italy's 2007 GDP was €1.5 trillion. The exchange rate between the euro and the US dollar averaged about $1.37 per euro that year. So in US dollars, Italy's 2007 GDP was $2.1 trillion.[2] If you use exchange rates to do the same conversion for all countries —or at least the largest of them—you can figure out how they all stack up.

Table 4.2 includes the nominal GDP of the 20 largest economies in the world in 2007, measured in US dollars. In the third column, you'll find each country's economic weight in the world.

Table 4.2   2007 GDP in USD

Country	2007 Nominal GDP in US Dollars (billions $)	Percent of World GDP
US	$13,844	25.5%
Japan	$4,384	8.1%
Germany	$3,322	6.1%
China	$3,251	6.0%
UK	$2,773	5.1%
France	$2,560	4.7%
Italy	$2,105	3.9%
Spain	$1,439	2.6%
Canada	$1,432	2.6%
Brazil	$1,314	2.4%
Russia	$1,290	2.4%
India	$1,099	2.0%
Korea	$957	1.8%
Australia	$909	1.7%
Mexico	$893	1.6%
Netherlands	$769	1.4%
Turkey	$663	1.2%
Sweden	$455	0.8%
Belgium	$454	0.8%
Indonesia	$433	0.8%

Source: International Monetary Fund.

You'll notice the US accounted for over a quarter of the world's economic output in 2007. That's impressive, but it's actually down from over 35 percent in the mid-1980s. That's not because the US economy is getting smaller. On the contrary, annual real US GDP growth has averaged better than 3 percent since then. But many foreign countries are growing much faster. All the more reason to look for investment opportunities outside the US!

These 20 countries account for over 80 percent of global GDP. So if you know these, you've got a pretty good handle on the big economic picture.

Or the Three Ps

Using PPP to compare GDP is somewhat more complicated because it involves comparing the cost of goods in different markets. PPP attempts to adjust the size of a country's economy for the amount of goods and services that economic output would allow citizens of that country to buy. Using exchange rates, one US dollar will buy you about seven Moroccan dirham.[3] If you want to get your hair cut, spending just five bucks in the US might put your locks in jeopardy, whereas 35 dirham in Morocco gets you a coiffure fit for a king.

Table 4.3 shows the sizes of the same 20 economies as Table 4.2. But the data is shown in *international dollars*. No, you didn't miss out on the introduction of a new global currency. The international dollar is a fictitious currency, conceived for the express purpose of determining PPP. Notice the difference between these values and those in Table 4.2.

Attempts to measure purchasing power have resulted in some interesting comparison tools. One of the more famous is the Big Mac Index developed by the folks at *The Economist*. There's also a Tall Latte Index. And where would we be in this digital age without an iPod Index? The purpose of all these whimsical measures is to take widely used products and compare their prices in different countries to evaluate currencies' purchasing power.

Table 4.3   2007 Global GDP Using Purchasing Power Parity (PPP)

Country	2007 Nominal GDP using PPP (in billions)	Percent of World PPP GDP
US	$13,675	19.3%
Japan	$4,346	6.1%
Germany	$2,645	3.7%
China	$11,207	15.8%
UK	$2,225	3.1%
France	$2,020	2.8%
Italy	$1,852	2.6%
Spain	$1,276	1.8%
Canada	$1,215	1.7%
Brazil	$1,805	2.5%
Russia	$1,877	2.6%
India	$4,555	6.4%
Korea	$1,229	1.7%
Australia	$718	1.0%
Mexico	$1,237	1.7%
Netherlands	$602	0.8%
Turkey	$708	1.0%
Sweden	$326	0.5%
Belgium	$380	0.5%
Indonesia	$1,038	1.5%

Source: International Monetary Fund.

Big Mac Index

From its humble beginnings in San Bernardino, California, McDonald's grew into the largest restaurant chain in the world. Each and every day, McDonald's serves burgers, fries, shakes, and other McGoodies to over 52 million customers in over 100 countries. One of McDonald's most popular offerings is the Big Mac. Big Macs are pretty similar no matter where they're served. ♪*Two all beef patties, special sauce, lettuce, cheese, pickles, onions on a sesame seed bun* ♪ (Now just try getting that jingle out of your head.)

The consistency and ubiquity of the Big Mac make it an interesting tool for comparing purchasing power in different countries. A Big Mac purchased in Estonia doesn't

(Continued)

necessarily cost the same as a Big Mac in New York City, even if you convert kroons to US dollars. If the exchange rate implied by the Big Mac Index is far different than the market exchange rate, the value of the currency and the country's economic output might be over- or understated. Or it might just be folks in that country need to lay off the fast food.

And the Winner Is . . .

Neither method of comparing economies is perfect. The exchange rate method suffers from the fact currency markets are frequently influenced by non-market forces. (Chapter 8 explains some of the forces impacting exchange rates). An undervalued currency means the value of everything a country produces might actually be greater than the exchange rate method suggests. Or it might be lower if the currency is overvalued.

PPP attempts to correct this problem, but it it's fraught with its own issues. For one thing, the same product shouldn't necessarily have the same price in every market. The costs of parts and labor aren't the same everywhere. Transport costs vary depending on where a product is made and where it's sold. Some governments place price controls on certain goods. And in a free market, prices are determined by supply and demand, which vary wildly from place to place. And PPP is fairly subjective—different statisticians use different methods to come up with PPP conversion rates, so the resulting data can vary quite a bit.

When choosing between the two, I prefer exchange rates. They're market-based (even if there is some tomfoolery in the market), exchange rate data are easily accessible, and there's a single, widely accepted exchange rate between most currencies.

TAKING STOCK . . . GLOBALLY

For a global investor, it's important to have a grasp of the economic landscape. But economics alone don't give you an inkling of where to invest. The sizes of countries' stock markets are even more important than the sizes of their economies.

Different countries have different capital structures, so there's no fixed relationship between the size of a country's economy and the size of its stock markets. Companies in some countries raise more capital by selling stocks than companies in other countries. It's that simple. A large, fast-growing economy doesn't necessarily mean that country's stock market will be either large or fast growing. Sometimes the exact opposite is true.

Leftover Chinese

China's economic growth has been nothing short of miraculous. According to the International Monetary Fund, 20 years ago, China's economy was the eighth largest in the world, trailing countries like Italy, Canada, and France. But over those 20 years, China has experienced tremendous growth.

Just a few decades ago, China's was a slow-moving, planned economy. The central government controlled everything from prices to production. But as China moved toward a market-based economy, many industries flourished. As you saw in Table 4.2, China now boasts the world's fourth-largest economy. Most estimates have China surpassing Germany in 2008, and some forecast China will be the world's largest economy by the middle of the century. With all this growth, you might expect China's stock market to have been *the* place to be invested.

Not exactly.

Table 4.4 shows real GDP growth and the return on the Shanghai A Shares Index in the 15 years to 2007. Economic growth has been blistering throughout, but stock market returns have been mixed. Some years have been great, others have been middling to miserable. From 2000 to 2005, China's economy grew at a stupendous average annual rate of 9.6 percent, while the stock market was floundering with average annual returns of negative 11.0 percent.

None of this matters much to non-Chinese investors because government controls prevent foreigners from owning most Chinese shares. Foreigners can buy shares of Chinese companies listed in Hong Kong. There are B-share markets on the mainland exchanges, which foreigners can access. And some Chinese companies have American Depository Receipts (aka ADRs; more on these in Chapter 7) trading here in the US. But for the most part, Chinese shares are off-limits.

(Continued)

Table 4.4   China's GDP Growth and Stock Market Returns

Year	Real GDP Growth	Shanghai A Local Currency Return
1993	14.0%	3.9%
1994	13.1%	−21.2%
1995	10.9%	−13.9%
1996	10.0%	66.0%
1997	9.3%	31.8%
1998	7.8%	−3.1%
1999	7.6%	19.0%
2000	8.4%	51.0%
2001	8.3%	−21.9%
2002	9.1%	−17.1%
2003	10.0%	10.6%
2004	10.1%	−15.2%
2005	10.4%	−8.2%
2006	11.6%	130.6%
2007	11.9%	96.1%

Source: Bloomberg Finance L.P.

So you see, even though the size and growth of an economy are important considerations when making investment decisions, there are many other factors at work.

The Big Picture

If you added up the economic output of every country and the value of every share of stock, the numbers are fairly similar. In total, the world churned out about $54 trillion in goods and services in 2007.[4] That's pretty close to the value of global stocks, which totaled about $60 trillion.[5] But there's no reason the two should be linked.

Economic output comes from a number of different sources, not just publicly traded firms. Privately held firms, governments, and a host of other organizations contribute to economic growth. And as pointed out repeatedly in this book, firms do business all over the world, so they're not limited by the size of their home economies. As a result, some countries' stock markets are large relative to the size of their economies. Others are relatively small.

Countries with developed economies have historically made greater use of capital markets than developing countries, so developed countries usually have larger stock markets.

But there are definitely exceptions to this rule. For example, Germany's economy is the largest in Europe, but Germany's stock market is relatively small. The value of all German stocks amounts to 66 percent of the size of

Developed or Emerging: Who Decides?

Markets and economies are frequently classified by their level of development. Some countries are considered *developed*. Others are *emerging*. And countries with the lowest level of economic development are frequently known as *frontier* markets.

The criteria used to classify markets vary depending on who's doing the classifying. But there are some common factors distinguishing one group from the other. You might be surprised to learn size isn't the primary consideration. Some of the largest economies are considered emerging. If you look at Table 4.2, you'll notice Brazil, Russia, India, and China (known as the BRIC countries among emerging-market investors) are among the largest economies in the world. Look ahead at Table 4.6 and you'll see they're also home to some of the largest stock markets. Yet these countries are almost universally considered emerging, while much smaller markets such as Sweden and the Netherlands are consider developed.

Depth of capital markets, political stability, openness to foreign investment, per capita economic output, and a host of other factors go into classifying countries. Since the criteria aren't universal, countries aren't always classified the same way. As you'll read in Chapter 6, countries such as South Korea and Israel are considered developed by some and emerging by others. And countries don't necessarily stay in one group. Country classifications can change as market and economic conditions evolve.

Emerging and frontier markets often pose some risks not often encountered in developed markets. As you'll read in Chapter 9, political systems can be unstable, capital markets are less developed, property rights sometimes aren't well established, and capital controls frequently inhibit foreign investment. So how a country is classified can have an impact on investor appetite for equities there. Some investors view emerging and frontier markets as particularly risky (which they can be), so they avoid stocks from

(Continued)

countries with those classifications. Others might specifically target stocks there, looking for hidden investment opportunities.

Emerging markets also provide some features not commonly found in the developed world. For example, stocks in emerging markets can be quite volatile. As mentioned above, emerging economies and markets tend to be less developed and diverse than developed economies and markets. When times are good, emerging markets really do emerge. But during tough times, emerging markets can find themselves submerging. The difference in the performance of emerging markets between 2007 and 2008 reflects this volatility. In 2007, emerging market stocks in aggregate outperformed developed market stocks by a long shot. But so far in 2008, emerging market stocks have reversed course, many giving up all their 2007 gains and then some. So on their own, emerging market stocks can carry some additional risk. But emerging market stocks have also tended to have relatively low correlations with stocks in developed markets. So as part of a global portfolio, emerging markets not only have high growth potential, they also offer additional diversification opportunities despite their higher volatility.

Chapter 6 shows emerging markets still make up a relatively small piece of global markets, but their importance for global investors is growing dramatically. Not only are many emerging economies growing faster than those of developed countries, firms based in these markets are becoming some of the largest in the world. As such, emerging and frontier should be approached cautiously, but they shouldn't be ignored.

the German economy.[6] By comparison, US stocks are 128 percent of the size of the US economy.[7] And UK stocks are worth a whopping 146 percent of the UK economy.[8] Additionally, many emerging economies' stock markets have been thriving in recent years, so the size of their markets relative to their economies have grown. Table 4.5 shows the size of various countries' stock markets relative to the sizes of their economies.

Domestic Market Capitalization

Armed with the countries' GDP and sizes of their economies relative to their stock markets, it's pretty easy to back into each country's *domestic market capitalization*. A country's weight in the global stock market is determined by the domestic market capitalization as a percent of all the world's stocks. The next chapter covers why knowing the sizes of countries' stock markets is an integral part of building a global portfolio.

Table 4.5 GDP and Market Capitalization

Country	Stock Market Capitalization as % of GDP
Switzerland	286%
Taiwan	183%
India	165%
Australia	156%
UK	146%
China	137%
US	128%
Sweden	127%
Canada	122%
Korea	115%
World	**112%**
France	107%
Brazil	106%
Norway	105%
Japan	104%
Belgium	89%
Russia	77%
Spain	76%
Netherlands	75%
Germany	66%
Italy	53%
Poland	50%
Indonesia	47%
Mexico	45%
Turkey	43%

Source: International Monetary Fund, Bloomberg Finance L.P.

These ratios aren't static. As you read previously in this chapter, some economies grow faster than others. But changes in the sizes of even the most dynamic economies can seem ho-hum compared to changes in the value of global stock markets stock market. So it's the market capitalization part of this equation that drives significant changes in countries' capital structures. For example, the severe downturn in global markets in 2008 caused the total value of global stocks to decline by about a third.[9] Yet the global economy continued to expand, albeit at a slower pace than in prior years. As a result, the data in Table 4.5 will undoubtedly look far different at the end of 2008 than it did at the end of 2007.

Definition

Domestic Market Capitalization

The size of a country's stock market can be measured by the country's *domestic market capitalization*. This is the market value of all a country's publicly traded domestic companies. It doesn't include mutual funds, exchange-traded funds, or foreign companies listed on a country's exchanges. To calculate domestic market capitalization, multiply the number of shares outstanding by the current share price for every domestic company. Add these together, and the total is the domestic market capitalization.

Table 4.6 shows the total market capitalizations of some of the largest equity markets in the world in 2007 in both US dollars and as a percent of global equity markets.

Table 4.6   Market Capitalization by Country

Country	Total Market Capitalization	Percent of World Market
World	$60,851	
US	$17,663	29.0%
Japan	$4,546	7.5%
China	$4,459	7.3%
UK	$4,047	6.7%
France	$2,737	4.5%
Germany	$2,207	3.6%
India	$1,815	3.0%
Canada	$1,749	2.9%
Australia	$1,413	2.3%
Brazil	$1,399	2.3%
Switzerland	$1,212	2.0%
Italy	$1,106	1.8%
Korea	$1,103	1.8%
Spain	$1,088	1.8%
Russia	$996	1.6%
Taiwan	$701	1.2%
Sweden	$577	0.9%
Netherlands	$575	0.9%
Saudi Arabia	$507	0.8%
Norway	$412	0.7%

Source: Bloomberg Finance L.P.

INDUSTRY CLASSIFICATION

Knowing where a firm is domiciled is immensely important because the market conditions in its home country will impact its stock price. But there are many different types of companies within each country. So it's just as important to know what types of firms comprise global equity markets. Why? For one thing, it helps to ensure proper diversification. You might own stocks from countries all over the world. But if they're all steelmakers and the price of steel plummets, your portfolio probably will, too. A well-built portfolio needs industry diversification as well as geographic diversification.

Classifying companies by the businesses they're in is challenging, but several systems have been developed to accomplish the task. Some are intended to classify companies in specific countries or regions. The North American Industry Classification System (NAICS) was developed by the US, Canada, and Mexico as a means of comparing business activities across North America. But global investors need a system classifying all types of companies all over the world. In this section, we'll introduce you to two of the most widely used classification systems suiting those needs.

GICS

The Global Industry Classification Standard (GICS) was developed in 1999 by Morgan Stanley Capital International (MSCI) and Standard & Poor's (S&P). GICS has a hierarchical structure consisting of four classification levels. The levels get increasingly granular, so each tells a little bit more about a company. The GICS system consists of 10 sectors, 24 industry groups, 68 industries, and 154 sub-industries. Table 4.7 includes the GICS structure for one sector—Consumer Discretionary. A similar structure exists for each sector in the GICS system.

Let's run through an example of how an actual company is classified. Most people are familiar with the Japanese firm Sony Corp. Sony makes a number of popular products including PlayStation videogame consoles and VAIO computers. These are considered discretionary items, so it's no wonder Sony falls into the Consumer Discretionary sector in GICS.

As you can see in Table 4.7, there are five different industry groups within the Consumer Discretionary sector: Automobiles &

Table 4.7 The Consumer Discretionary Sector in GICS

Sector	Industry Group	Industry	Sub-Industry
Consumer Discretionary	Automobiles & Components	Auto Components	Auto Parts & Equipment Tires & Rubber
		Automobiles	Automobile Manufacturers Motorcycle Manufacturers
	Consumer Durables & Apparel	Household Durables	Consumer Electronics Home Furnishings Homebuilding Household Appliances Housewares & Specialties
		Leisure Equipment & Products	Leisure Products Photographic Products
		Textiles, Apparel, & Luxury Goods	Apparel, Accessories, & Luxury Goods Footwear Textiles
	Consumer Services	Hotels, Restaurants, & Leisure	Casinos & Gaming Hotels, Resorts, & Cruise Lines Leisure Facilities Restaurants
		Diversified Consumer Services	Education Services Specialized Consumer Services
	Media	Media	Advertising Broadcasting Cable & Satellite Movies & Entertainment Publishing
	Retailing	Distributors	Distributors
		Internet & Catalog Retail	Catalog Retail Internet Retail
		Multiline Retail	Department Stores General Merchandise Stores
		Specialty Retail	Apparel Retail Computer & Electronics Retail Home Improvement Retail Specialty Stores Automotive Retail Homefurnishing Retail

Source: MSCI, Inc.[10]

Components, Consumer Durables & Apparel, Consumer Services, Media, and Retailing. Although Sony undoubtedly has some over-lapping business lines (for instance, if Sony Pictures were a stand-alone company, it would probably fall into the Media industry group), the bulk of its business puts it in the Consumer Durables & Apparel industry group. This industry group is broken down into three industries, each of which gives you a little more insight into a company's business. Sony is in the Household Durables indus-try. Finally, this industry is further divided into five sub-industries, including the Consumer Electronics sub-industry, which contains Sony.

ICB.   The Industry Classification Benchmark (ICB) has similar characteristics to GICS, but the structure and methodology aren't quite the same. Like GICS, ICB has four levels. These include 10 industries, 18 supersectors, 39 sectors, and 104 subsectors. Table 4.8 shows the ICB structure for the Consumer Goods industry.

Now back to Sony. Again, it's not surprising to see Sony in the Consumer Goods industry in ICB. There are three supersectors in this industry. Sony falls in Personal & Household Goods. This supersector is divided into four sectors: Household Goods & Home Construction, Leisure Goods, Personal Goods, and Tobacco. ICB puts Sony in the Leisure Goods. There are three subsectors in this sec-tor. Sony lands in the Consumer Electronics subsector.

The Problem with Conglomerates.   Classifying firms by their busi-nesses can be tricky. Some firms are trickier than others. Your local regional bank is probably just that—a bank. It's unlikely they run a supermarket on the side or sell cosmetics when the bank is closed. But putting some firms in a specific category can be challenging. This is especially true for some of the largest firms with multiple divisions in many, often dissimilar, businesses.

Consider General Electric (GE). In 2007, GE was the second-largest US firm and the world's third largest.[11] GE has a commercial finance division, an industrial division, an infrastructure division, a

Table 4.8   The Consumer Goods Industry in ICB

Industry	Supersector	Sector	Subsector
Consumer Goods	Automobiles & Parts	Automobiles & Parts	Automobiles Auto Parts Tires
	Food & Beverage	Beverages	Brewers Distillers & Vintners Soft Drinks
		Food Producers	Farming & Fishing Food Products
	Personal & Household Goods	Household Goods & Home Construction	Durable Household Products Nondurable Household Products Furnishings Home Construction
		Leisure Goods	Consumer Electronics Recreational Products Toys
		Personal Goods	Clothing & Accessories Footwear Personal Products
		Tobacco	Tobacco

Source: Industry Classification Benchmark.

consumer finance division, a healthcare division, and an entertainment division (NBC Universal). So it isn't easy to put a firm like GE in a single, specific category. Still, even conglomerates have places in GICS and ICB. But even the most specific categories aren't too revealing about these companies' businesses. They can't be. The companies are just too diverse. Table 4.9 shows how GE is classified under both systems.

Which classification system is better? Neither really. In the next chapter, you'll learn some stock indexes use GICS and some use ICB. Similarly, there are exchange-traded and mutual funds designed using GICS and ICB. The most important thing is to consistently use one or the other to avoid gaps and overlaps in your portfolio.

Table 4.9   GE in GICS and ICB

GICS		
	Sector	Industrials
	Industry Group	Capital Goods
	Industry	Industrial Conglomerates
	Sub-industry	Industrial Conglomerates
ICB		
	Industry	Industrials
	Super Sector	Industrial Goods & Services
	Sector	General Industrials
	Subsector	Diversified Industrials

Source: Bloomberg Finance L.P.

Crossing the Intersection

Knowing company locales and classifications are essential pieces of information. But they're most useful when you consider them together. Greek software companies and Greek utilities don't act alike just because they're Greek, so knowing the country isn't enough. And Singaporean and Russian pharmaceutical companies don't act alike just because they all make drugs.

Table 4.10 shows the intersection between the 23 developed countries and the 10 sectors in the GICS classification system. ("n/a"s appear where MSCI does not produce indexes for a particular country/sector intersection.) The countries are along the vertical axis. The sectors are at the top along the horizontal axis. The squares in between show the return for each intersection in 2007. There are some big differences in the performance of different sectors within each country. There are also big differences in each sector among stocks from different countries.

If all your Financials stocks were located in the US, that part of your portfolio had a pretty bad year. But if some were located in Greece, Australia, and Hong Kong, you probably fared better. The same goes for sectors within countries. Overall, Japanese stocks did poorly in 2007, but the Energy and Industrials sectors posted pretty good returns.

Table 4.10   Country/Sector Intersections

Country	Sector									
	Energy	Materials	Industrials	Consumer Discretionary	Consumer Staples	Health Care	Financials	Information Technology	Telecommunications Services	Utilities
Australia	45.1%	59.1%	17.3%	6.4%	37.5%	59.7%	15.3%	25.1%	34.2%	4.5%
Austria	45.3%	23.8%	3.4%	81.7%	n/a	n/a	−17.3%	n/a	6.8%	33.6%
Belgium	24.5%	9.5%	39.0%	−15.8%	19.5%	−34.2%	−8.4%	−13.9%	16.2%	n/a
Canada	28.5%	56.9%	30.8%	20.9%	7.6%	−19.4%	13.9%	80.7%	40.5%	33.8%
Denmark	23.2%	33.6%	60.0%	−25.1%	4.4%	37.3%	−6.0%	n/a	n/a	n/a
Finland	19.2%	−9.5%	9.0%	36.0%	7.4%	12.6%	4.4%	89.7%	22.1%	65.1%
France	18.2%	47.9%	16.2%	11.4%	28.9%	3.6%	−4.2%	−25.3%	34.6%	30.0%
Germany	n/a	53.5%	51.1%	57.0%	23.5%	20.7%	13.4%	−3.0%	25.7%	49.8%
Greece	11.4%	−6.3%	23.7%	9.4%	67.9%	n/a	37.4%	n/a	28.3%	109.5%
Hong Kong	n/a	−52.7%	13.6%	27.5%	n/a	n/a	62.0%	17.2%	−2.1%	20.9%
Ireland	n/a	−14.8%	−33.3%	11.2%	−23.5%	52.6%	−27.9%	n/a	n/a	n/a
Italy	12.7%	−23.0%	23.8%	3.4%	n/a	n/a	0.5%	n/a	5.4%	21.0%
Japan	13.6%	0.4%	7.8%	−5.8%	−1.1%	−6.2%	−19.3%	3.4%	6.7%	−12.0%
Netherlands	19.4%	22.8%	0.3%	14.6%	39.2%	n/a	10.6%	21.5%	32.9%	n/a
New Zealand	n/a	17.6%	49.5%	−0.7%	n/a	−7.2%	0.4%	n/a	7.4%	9.2%
Norway	24.8%	25.0%	79.1%	22.6%	−27.9%	n/a	9.2%	41.7%	29.0%	n/a
Portugal	n/a	7.1%	28.6%	10.6%	79.1%	n/a	17.9%	n/a	23.0%	31.9%
Singapore	105.6%	n/a	49.8%	27.1%	77.5%	41.5%	16.9%	−0.9%	38.1%	n/a
Spain	5.4%	−17.1%	7.3%	6.8%	32.9%	21.5%	11.8%	14.5%	57.1%	38.6%
Sweden	−10.1%	−9.1%	13.2%	12.7%	32.2%	8.7%	3.5%	−41.0%	29.3%	n/a
Switzerland	n/a	18.0%	35.0%	21.5%	31.5%	−2.0%	−13.0%	1.3%	6.0%	n/a
UK	24.0%	57.5%	4.6%	−12.9%	26.9%	−4.7%	−14.4%	−15.7%	29.6%	13.8%
US	35.9%	27.8%	12.8%	−11.6%	13.5%	6.0%	−19.2%	16.7%	10.4%	18.1%

Source: Thomson Datastream, MSCI, Inc.[12]

The Global View

Like continents riding on tectonic plates, global economic and market landscapes are continually changing. Twenty years ago, global economies and markets looked vastly different than they do today. Japan had the world's largest equity markets, and countries like China and Brazil were economic afterthoughts. Today, Japanese markets comprise a much smaller portion of global equity markets than it did then, and China and Brazil are economic powerhouses. Twenty years from now, the global landscape will likely have evolved again.

Some economies are growing by leaps and bounds. Some aren't. Some stock markets are expanding. Some aren't doing much at all. The information given here is merely a snapshot in time. Global investing is an ongoing exercise, so be sure to keep abreast of how the landscape is changing.

Top-Down
Investing

T here comes a time when you must choose a side. Aisle or window? Boxers or briefs? Bottled or tap? Paper or plastic? Hatfields or McCoys? Investing is no exception. If you had to break investing down into two main disciplines, some would be *bottom-up* investors and others *top-down*. Not everyone falls into these categories. Technicians read charts like tea leaves, hoping to spot trends to exploit. And quantitative investors plug endless amounts of data into computers to glean investment ideas. But most of us without mystical powers or advanced programming skills fall into the bottom-up or top-down categories.

ARE YOU DOWN FOR BOTTOM-UP
OR UP FOR TOP-DOWN?

Many people don't know which group they belong to because few know the difference. Bottom-up sounds like an invitation to polish off a pint of ale rather than an investing strategy. And top-down could have more to do with convertible cars than investing. But the

81

difference between bottom-up and top-down is related to how you make investment decisions.

Definition

Bottom-Up and Top-Down

Bottom-up is an investing discipline in which investors focus primarily on specific individual investments rather than higher-level factors such as the macroeconomic environment. *Top-down* is an investing discipline that puts higher-level factors such as macroeconomic conditions ahead of individual investments.

If you spend most of your time hunting for hot stocks, you fall into the bottom-up camp. If you consider countries and sectors before even thinking about picking a stock, you're leaning toward the top-down group. And if the first question you ask yourself is "Should I own stocks at all?" there's a good chance you're a dyed-in-the-wool top-downer.

As you probably guessed, bottom-up investors put the most emphasis on picking stocks. They scour the investment universe for a handful of gems for their portfolios. From a global perspective, this means sorting through roughly 25,000 investable stocks to find a few dozen good candidates—a daunting task to say the least. The type of stock is usually an afterthought. It could be a grocery store, an auto parts maker, a fertilizer producer, or an Internet start-up. The company could be located in Toledo or Timbuktu. Highly orthodox bottom-up investors judge companies exclusively on their own merits with little, if any, regard for stocks' broader characteristics.

The top-down approach is different. Top-down investors make the highest-level decisions first, letting economic and market conditions guide their investment choices. If the environment looks good for stocks (which it usually does, considering the stock market rises about 65 percent of the time),[1] that's where top-down investors want to put their money. Once they've decided on an asset allocation, they choose what types of stocks they want to buy. From the many countries, sectors, and styles, they decide which they think will do best. Will Telecom stocks outperform Industrials? Will micro-cap stocks outperform mega-cap stocks? Will Dutch stocks outperform Swedish stocks? Only after these decisions have been made do top-down investors begin picking individual companies to invest in—if they do at all. As explained later, some top-down investors might decide not to own any individual stocks—an unthinkable idea for the bottom-up crowd.

Most in the financial services industry utilize the bottom-up approach. MBAs and CFAs are trained in bottom-up methodology. Broker-dealers hire these bottom-uppers as investment bankers and analysts who take companies public and produce prodigious amounts of bottom-up research. They create earnings models and make assumptions about discounted cash flows. They analyze inventories and pipelines and leverage ratios. Brokers then peddle individual stocks to their clients based on bottom-up recommendations. The industry was built from the bottom-up, and it's been a good business model. But that doesn't mean it's right for every investor.

TOP-DOWN IS TOPS

I don't mean to disparage bottom-up investing entirely. Many professional investors have been extremely successful investing from the bottom-up. But I think a top-down approach gives most investors the best chance of achieving their investment objectives. Top-down investing has characteristics that make it a better choice for most people.

Focus. The top-down approach enables investors to concentrate their resources in the areas they believe will be most fruitful. No investor has the capacity to research every stock on the planet. Even the largest brokerage firms and asset managers don't come close. Granted, you don't have to research *every* stock to find some that will do well. But how do investors

How Many Needles in Your Haystack?

Picking stocks that beat the market isn't easy. And building a portfolio of stocks that consistently outperforms the market is even more challenging. But you've got a decided leg up if you pick from a pool of stocks that generally performs better.

In 2007, the S&P 500 returned 5.5 percent. Of the 500 index members, 54 percent did better than the index. So if you picked US stocks at random, you had a little better than a 50/50 chance each would outperform the market. But what if you were searching in a haystack that had more needles? The best performing developed countries in 2007 were Finland (+48.7 percent), Hong Kong (+41.2 percent), and Germany (+35.2 percent). If your haystack was located in Finland, 65 percent of stocks there did better than the S&P 500. In Hong Kong, 74 percent of stocks outpaced the S&P. And in Germany, 75 percent beat the US index.

The same holds for sectors. If you were choosing among global energy stocks, 82 percent outperformed the S&P 500. There were also quite a few needles in the Utilities sector, where 73 percent outperformed.

Getting those top-down decisions right is even more important than acing your stock selection because you'll have a much better chance of consistently picking winners.

Source: Thomson Datastream, MSCI Inc.[2]

decide where to focus efforts? That's where the top-down approach comes in. Instead of trying to pick a few needles out of the colossal global haystack, top-down investors choose areas of the market they expect to do best, honing in on the haystacks with the most needles.

Risk control. Top-down investing also makes it much easier to control risk. Pure bottom-up investing ignores the types of stocks purchased, so the bottom-up approach can easily result in unintended concentrations in certain types of stocks. For instance, bottom-up investors might own too many technology stocks. If technology companies have a miserable year like they did in 2001, 2002, 2004, and 2006, when technology

Forget About Stocks???

Earlier I mentioned top-down investors can decide *not to own any stocks at all*. This concept might seem out of place in a book about building a global stock portfolio, but hear me out. Today, it's easy to get global stock market exposure without owning shares of individual stocks. As you'll read in Chapter 7, there are thousands of mutual funds and exchange-traded funds (ETFs) available, allowing you to eschew stock picking but still invest in stocks.

Most mutual fund and ETF investors utilize a top-down technique, even if their fund managers don't. Just about every fund has some kind of mandate. They might invest in US stocks, or foreign, or stocks ending in the letter "Y," or stocks with names that rhyme. Whatever the mandate, fund investors (whether they know it or not) make top-down decisions about the type of stocks they want to own. Even investors choosing the broadest funds intended to track the whole market are making the highest level, top-down decision to get exposure to stocks.

A stock-free portfolio isn't a great option for everyone—it can be very costly and inefficient, particularly for investors with larger amounts to invest—but the ability to invest globally without individual stocks does mean just about anyone can enjoy the benefits of global investing. (Chapter 7 will provide additional insight on when owning individual stocks does and doesn't make sense.)

was the worst performing sector,[3] all those technology stocks greatly increase your chance of lagging the market.

Because top-down investors consider the types of stocks they're buying before the stocks themselves, they can better control their exposure to different investment areas.

Top-down and bottom-up investors needn't be mortal enemies. In fact, elements of both top-down and bottom-up investing exist in symbiotic oneness in most portfolios. Top-down investors who buy individual stocks have to incorporate some bottom-up analysis, or they might as well pick stocks out of a hat. And some higher-level decisions undoubtedly make their way into the bottom-up investor's psyche. It's really the priority of your decision-making that puts you in one category or the other.

THE TOP-DOWN PROCESS

Later, I'll examine some of the elements that should factor into your top-down decisions, but before you jump headlong into top-down analysis, you need to know how the top-down process works.

There's a distinct hierarchy to top-down investing. All your investment decisions are important, but as I mentioned earlier, top-down investing starts with decisions that should have the greatest impact on your portfolio's performance looking forward.

In all, there are three steps to top-down investing, which we'll explore in the rest of this chapter:

1. Asset allocation.
2. Sub-asset allocation.
3. Stock picking.

STEP 1: ASSET ALLOCATION

The first and most important decision a top-down investor makes is which asset class to invest in. This means choosing your mix of stocks, bonds, and cash. This book's unabashed bias toward owning stocks is undoubtedly already apparent (and will become increasingly so shortly), so you won't be shocked to find the top-down process beginning from an all-equity perspective. But the process works just as well if you find you do need to own some bonds, though some of the steps and the factors you consider will differ.

As explained in Chapter 1, to choose the overall asset allocation most appropriate for you requires knowing a few things about your personal situation—most importantly, your investment objectives, the investing time horizon, and your cash flow needs. While every investor differs, and I can't know your specifics, it's apparent most investors generally should own more stocks and less bonds and cash than they think.

For most investors who want growth, stocks should comprise most, if not all, of their portfolio (unless they have short time horizons or need their portfolios to generate significant amounts of cash flow).

In general, bonds serve one purpose—to reduce volatility. The downside is they also have far less growth potential. Many investors mistakenly think they need bonds for the regular coupon payments, but you needn't rely on tax-inefficient coupon payments for income. Contrary to what most investors believe, stocks can be more efficient at producing cash than bonds.

You Don't Need Fixed Income to Get Income

Bonds have a reputation as the investment of choice for people needing to regularly draw cash from their portfolios. Even the moniker "fixed income" suggests bonds are tailor-made for this purpose. But when most investors say they need "income" from their investments, what they really mean is they need "cash flow," and bonds might not be the best way to get it.

Bonds generate consistent income, but that income comes at a price. As highlighted in Chapter 1, stocks do better than bonds over just about any significant time period, so investors with long time horizons give up quite a bit of growth to get income from bonds.

Bonds are also tax inefficient. Corporate and Treasury bond coupon payments are usually taxable as ordinary income. And municipal bond yields are generally well below those of taxable bonds to compensate for their tax-free status.

Instead, why not turn to stocks for cash flow? Investors can get the cash they need from an all-stock portfolio in a couple of ways. One way is through dividend payments. Many companies pay dividends and most are taxed at a lower rate than bond coupon payments. (However, some dividends don't receive preferential tax treatment, such as those paid by Real Estate Investment Trusts.) Dividends are issued on a discretionary basis whereas bond coupon payments are usually mandatory, so there is some risk a company will cut its dividend, although most healthy companies are extremely reluctant to do so.

Fortunately, there's an even better way to get cash from a stock portfolio—sell stocks! Long-term capital gains tax rates are normally lower than tax rates on interest payments. And gains can often be offset with losses, greatly lessening your tax liability. In some cases, your access to cash might be tax free!

It's wise for investors needing cash flow to keep some cash on hand at all times—maybe a few months worth of distributions—but don't let too much cash or fixed income become a drag on your portfolio or cause you to send too much of your money to Uncle Sam.

Be Dynamic

Top-down investing is inherently dynamic. Starting out with an all-stock portfolio doesn't mean you have to be perpetually invested in stocks. Even though stocks are almost always your best bet over the long term, stocks do experience significant periods of decline.

Definition

Bull Market, Bear Market, and Correction

The terms *bull market*, *bear market*, and *market correction* define different types of market movements. A bull market is a period of generally rising prices for an extended period of time. A bear market is the opposite—a period of generally falling prices. A 20 percent rise or fall is the magnitude commonly used to define a bull or bear market, but there's more to it than just the magnitude of the move.

A sharp 20 percent decline—give or take a bit—from which the market recovers quickly doesn't really qualify as a bear market. Nor does a 20 percent rally followed by extended declines. True bull and bear markets need both magnitude and duration.

A market correction is a meaningful market move against the prevailing trend that doesn't qualify as a bull or a bear. A 15 percent drop in prices during a bull market would be a correction, as would a 15 percent increase in prices during a bear market.

If you see a bear market coming, you can change your asset class for a time to try to avoid some of the downturn. That means moving out of stocks into bonds, cash, or both. But do so with extreme caution and only if you have some expertise in forecasting bear markets. Bear markets aren't easy to spot before they happen. If they were, they'd probably never occur because investors would be expecting them and would do their selling ahead of time. And more often than not, what investors believe is an oncoming bear usually turns out to be a modest downturn or a correction—neither of which warrants making changes to your asset allocation.

Recipe for a Bear

Looking ahead now, no one can tell you when the next bear market is coming or how big it will be. But there are some factors accompanying typical bear markets you can look out for. The recipe for most bear markets is fairly simple. Only two ingredients are required, but together they pack a punch.

Ingredient 1: An Unforeseen Negative Fundamental Event

This can be just about anything, but it has to be big. Monetary policy errors by a big central bank or banks, fiscal policy missteps, trade policy flubs, any number of geopolitical happenings, or regulatory blunders could all do the job—as long as the market doesn't see them coming. The stock market discounts widely known information, so if most investors have an inkling any of these events are approaching, their effects on the market are diffused right away.

Ingredient 2: Euphoric Sentiment

If you were investing at the turn of the millennium, you know a thing or two about euphoric sentiment. As the stock market roared into 2000, the talk was about a "new economy." Old rules like "companies should have earnings" and "I shouldn't buy dog food over the Internet just because a sock puppet tells me to" didn't apply. In an irrational environment where investors don't see any risk, most have already bought all the stocks they can. And the greediest have borrowed money to buy more. Mix these ingredients together, and you could be baking, sautéing, poaching, frying, or otherwise cooking up a bear market.

But remember: these are the ingredients for a *typical* bear market. Some bear markets are decidedly atypical. Sentiment was far from euphoric before the bear market that began in 2007, for example, but global stocks still suffered dramatic declines. Don't assume you'll always see bear markets coming. On the contrary, identifying a bear market before it happens is extremely difficult, even with the aforementioned ingredients in mind.

But be careful not to let overly cautious investing decisions sink your investing soufflé. After all, prognosticators are continually forecasting doom and gloom, but it rarely comes. The biggest mistake you can make as a global investor is to sell all your stocks in anticipation of a bear market that doesn't show up. Stocks do better than bonds or cash even with the big drops thrown in. It almost always pays to err on the side of caution and stay invested.

STEP 2: SUB-ASSET ALLOCATION

You've decided you want to own stocks. Good move. Now it's on to the second step in the top-down process: Deciding what types of stocks to own. We call this sub-asset allocation.

Many investors are familiar with the process of choosing an asset allocation. But choosing a *sub-asset allocation* is a more common concern for top-down investors than it is for bottom-up folks. Once an investor has decided to own stocks (the asset allocation decision), the sub-asset allocation refers to the types of stocks investors decide to own. Favoring health-care stocks over industrial stocks is a sub-asset allocation decision as is favoring Italian stocks over Finnish stocks or small stocks over large stocks. Stocks come in a multitude of different flavors. In the previous chapter, I discussed the various countries, sectors, and industries to choose from, but there are other dimensions as well, known as *styles*. You can choose between large stocks and small stocks, growth stocks and value stocks, domestically focused stocks and multinationals, and any combination of these. If you expect large, growth-oriented exporters from Hong Kong to do well, I guarantee you'll find a few companies fitting the bill.

There are three main factors that should drive your sub-asset allocation decision: economic drivers, political drivers, and sentiment drivers.

Economic Drivers

The economic environment is one factor to consider when deciding where to invest. This applies to sectors and industries as well as countries. Some economic factors are local, others are global. Strong global economic growth might have you optimistic about companies producing basic materials as demand for commodities rises throughout the world, but high inflation in a particular country might temper your enthusiasm for stocks there.

To give you an idea of what to look for, I'll briefly touch on a couple of economic factors to monitor, but the few mentioned here represent a minute fraction of the economic data available. I skipped GDP since it was covered in Chapter 4, but GDP definitely belongs on the list of meaningful economic statistics.

Interest rates.   Virtually every country has two key interest rates. *Short-term* interest rates are set by a country's central bank. *Long-term* interest rates are usually the yields on long-term government debt and determined by the open market.

Central bankers fidget with short-term rates to keep money cheap enough to promote economic growth, but not so cheap as to stoke inflation. In the US, the Federal Open Market Committee (FOMC) decides on a *target rate* or *range* for overnight loans. This is the rate banks pay for borrowing money in the Federal funds market. Other central banks operate similarly. The Bank of England's Monetary Policy Committee (MPC) sets the *base rate* (aka *repo rate*) for the UK. The Bank of Japan's Policy Board determines the overnight *call rate*. The European Central Bank's Governing Council sets three key rates for the euro area: the *marginal lending facility rate*, the *deposit facility rate*, and the *main refinancing operations rate* (this is the most important and most often quoted of the three).

Fed Funds

Banks are known as places to go when you need a loan. But sometimes banks themselves need to borrow money. Most banks operate under a *fractional-reserve* system. When banks collect deposits in customers' checking accounts, savings accounts, certificates of deposit, and so on, they don't hold on to all that money. Instead, they keep a fraction (hence the name *fractional-reserve*) and invest or lend the rest.

On any given day, some banks will have reserves in excess of what's required, and some banks will need to borrow money to meet the reserve requirement. The banks with excess reserves would like to earn some interest on those funds. And those that need reserves don't mind paying a little interest to bring their reserves up to snuff. That's what the fed funds market is for.

In the fed funds market, banks with extra reserves lend to banks needing reserves. Most of these transactions are extremely short-term, usually overnight. Banks often lend money through what's known as a *repurchase (repo) agreement.* In a repo, banks needing money sell securities for a set period of time after which they buy the securities back.

In order to keep rates near its target rate, the Fed conducts *open market operations* in the fed funds market. If actual interest rates (known as the *effective* fed funds rate) rise above the target rate, the Fed lends additional money to bring rates down. If rates get too low, the Fed borrows money to bring rates up.

Central banks usually don't have the same influence over long-term interest rates, so these are set by market participants. Many factors influence long-term rates. One of the most important is inflation expectations. If investors expect high inflation, they're likely to demand higher yields on bonds because inflation eats away at the real return on their investments. You probably wouldn't buy a bond paying 3 percent for the next 10 years if you expect inflation to run at 4 percent. You'd be earning a negative real return!

Investor appetite for risk can also be a factor in determining long-term rates. Will Rogers once said he was more concerned about the return *of* his money than the return *on* his money. (If you're concerned about the latter, doesn't that mean you're also concerned about the former? I digress.) Like-minded investors sometimes seek the safety of government bonds, driving prices up and yields down (with bonds, prices and yields move in opposite directions). However, a rush to the safety of bonds doesn't have a long-lasting impact since fickle investors can abandon bonds just as quickly as they embraced them.

Both short-term and long-term interest rates are important to global investors. Short-term rates indicate the amount of liquidity being supplied to an economy. Long-term rates reflect the long-term cost

How Long Is Long-Term?

When investors ponder long-term interest rates, they're usually thinking of the yield on 10-year government bonds. This is the rate most commonly considered the "long-term" rate (by contrast, "short-term" rates are usually those banks charge each other for very short-term loans). But there are bonds with longer maturities. In 2006, the US began issuing 30-year bonds after more than a four-year hiatus. Several countries have issued 50-year bonds in recent years, including the UK, France, and Poland. A few corporations issue ultra-long-term bonds as well.

Who wants this long-term debt? Mostly investors with long-term obligations who are required to keep their money in bonds. (Not everyone is as well versed in the benefits of stocks ownership as you now are.) This includes some pensions, insurance firms, endowments, and others.

of money and give you an idea how quickly investors expect prices to rise. Additionally, stocks compete with long-term bonds for investment dollars, so long-term rates are particularly important.

Yield curve.   I mentioned short-term rates and long-term rates, but what about all those rates in between? Governments issue bonds for different periods, and once a bond is issued, the time until it matures changes constantly. The *yield curve* is simply a graphical representation of the yields on bonds with different maturities. Figure 5.1 shows a typical (positively sloped) yield curve.

Normally, longer maturity bonds have higher yields than shorter maturity bonds. That's because investors usually take on more risk lending money for longer periods, for example:

- Default risk—the chance borrowers don't pay up (even governments).
- Interest rate risk—if interest rates rise, the value of existing fixed-rate bonds decline.
- Opportunity cost—the likely chance other investments prove superior.

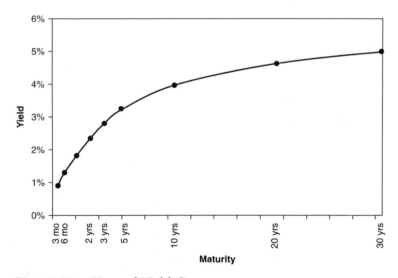

Figure 5.1   Normal Yield Curve

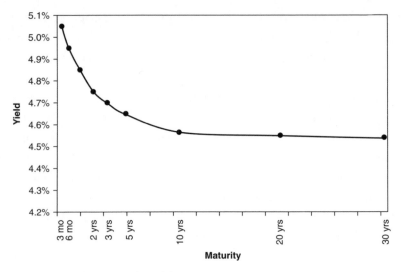

Figure 5.2   Inverted Yield Curve

The more time until a bond matures, the more risk, so investors usually require higher yields on bonds with longer maturities.

However, the yield curve will occasionally invert like the one in Figure 5.2. When a yield curve is inverted, short maturity bonds offer higher yields than long maturity bonds.

A *normal yield curve* is considered bullish for the economy because it creates an incentive for banks to lend money. Banks typically pay depositors or borrow money at rates at the short end of the yield curve, but they lend money at the long end. Think of the difference banks pay on savings accounts versus those they collect on mortgages (or any other type of loan). Usually, the latter is meaningfully higher than the former. The difference (or the spread) is the amount banks pocket.

A *steep yield curve* (meaning long-term interest rates are much higher than short-term interest rates) means banks earn a lot of money making loans, so they have a strong incentive to lend. This makes cash readily available to businesses and individuals. By contrast, an inverted yield curve squeezes interest margins, so banks don't lend as enthusiastically. But despite what you might read, an inverted yield curve doesn't mean the world is coming to an end.

Whenever a yield curve inverts, doomsayers come out of the wood-work suggesting it's time to pack up the family and go live in a cave until the yield curve gets back to normal. An inverted yield curve might not be a big plus, but it's hardly a harbinger of the apocalypse either. Banks typically lend at rates higher than government bond rates since their borrowers are less creditworthy than the government, so the yield curve isn't a perfect representation of the lending environment. And these days, banks have access to capital markets around the world, so they can borrow and lend wherever the environment is most favorable.

Economic drivers needn't and shouldn't be confined to things affecting a country's economy. After all, you're most concerned about the outlook for stocks, not the economy (as explained, there's a differ-ence). Also keep an eye out for things like mergers and acquisitions (M&A) and share buybacks. Even equity valuations are a higher-level theme when you consider them on a broad scale. Table 5.1 includes a few economic measures to keep on your radar.

Global Yield Curve

Clearly, it's easier than ever for investors to go global. But we're not the only ones reap-ing the rewards of a wide global reach. As mentioned in Chapter 1, businesses of all kinds are looking for opportunities overseas. Money flows more freely among countries as well, so even if the lending environment isn't ideal in one country, companies can find more favorable conditions abroad. Rather than focusing exclusively on the yield curve of a single country, investors also need to consider the global yield curve.

Short-term interest rates in countries like Japan, Switzerland, and even the US have recently been much lower than rates in Australia, New Zealand, and the UK. So banks can borrow money in countries with low rates and lend money in countries with higher rates.

If you recognize this exposes a company to exchange rate risk, you're a step ahead of the lessons in Chapter 8. But many banks and other companies can breathe easy when it comes to exchange rates because they generate revenue all over the world. If an Australian firm borrows money in Japan, converts it to Australian dollars, and lends money in Australia, a rising yen impacts the firm's profitability because the size of the loan increases in Australian dollars. But the effect is mitigated if the bank earns money in Japan, too. If it does, the value of the earnings goes up with the yen, offsetting the hit the bank takes on the loan.

(Continued)

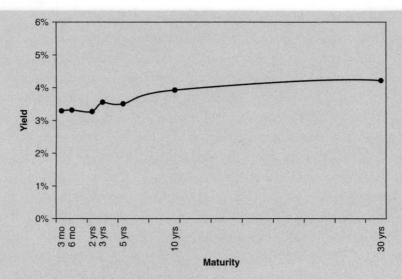

Figure 5.3   Global Yield Curve

Source: Bloomberg Finance L.P., International Monetary Fund.

Figure 5.3 shows a GDP weighted global yield curve as of March 31, 2008. This is fairly easy to construct. Simply add up the products of each country's interest rate and its share of global GDP. Do this for all maturities along the yield curve, and you've got a global yield curve. You'll do fine sticking to the largest developed countries since capital flows most freely among them (some emerging economies have capital controls inhibiting the free flow of money in and out).

Using just US, Japan, UK, Australia, New Zealand, and Eurozone rates, you'll cover 75 percent of the global economy, which is pretty good and much easier than trying to include everything down to Burundi. (Chances are, not many global banks are turning to Burundi for cash anyway.)

Table 5.1   Examples of Economic Drivers

Yield Curve	Inflation	M&A Activity
Relative GDP Growth	Bank Lending	Share Buybacks
Productivity	Infrastructure Spending	Export Growth
Relative Interest Rates	Monetary Policy	Employment

Political Drivers

Most economic drivers are quantifiable. If the government measures it, you can get the data, turn them into fancy charts and tables, and compare those to other fancy charts and tables. Employment, prices, productivity, money supply—the government releases data on all these economic measures and many, many more. Most of the data aren't perfectly consistent from country to country. For instance, the basket of goods in China's consumer price index might be vastly different than that of Iceland. But similar measures are at least roughly comparable.

Political drivers often aren't quite so straightforward. Political structures and policies can and usually do vary dramatically from country to country. The world is a hodgepodge of republics, kingdoms, commonwealths, federations, unions, and emirates. There's even a Jamahiriya (Libya) and a grand duchy (Luxembourg). And government systems are just as diverse, so you can't expect political drivers to be quite as consistent as even the oft disparate economic measures.

But some universal truisms exist even in politics. There are two things investors universally hate about politics: change and the prospect of change. Big political changes bring the potential for wealth redistribution, and there's nothing investors hate more. When governments redistribute wealth, some people get money and some people lose it. But the people who lose it are usually more upset than those that got it. So the net effect is almost always a less cheery group overall.

As with just about everything, there are exceptions to these rules. Change that takes power away from the government and gives it to capitalists usually draws the most cheers from investors. This includes things like tax cuts, pro-growth reforms, privatization, deregulation, and so on.

An example: In 2005, then Prime Minister Junichiro Koizumi dissolved Japan's lower house of parliament in an attempt to implement much needed pro-growth reforms. Koizumi was trying to push through a bill privatizing Japan's postal system (which included the enormous postal savings system), converting lumbering public institutions holding hundreds of trillions of yen into private corporations. The bill had been voted down in the upper house, so Koizumi's only hope was to attain a large enough majority in the more powerful lower house to override the upper-house vote. His gamble paid off and the bill passed. Investors expressed their approval by buying up shares. Japan's Topix index returned 45 percent in 2005 (but only 26 percent for US investors as the yen fell).[4]

Sentiment Drivers

Measuring sentiment is as much art as science. The mood ring was a valiant effort, but as far as we know, no one has developed a tool to accurately gauge the collective disposition of consumers, investors, businesses, or anyone else.

Even if such a wondrous invention did exist, it wouldn't presage future stock performance. People's moods tend to reflect how they feel at present or how they've felt in the past. No one can tell you how they will feel in 6 or 12 months because no one knows. You might plan on being chipper, only to have a hangnail ruin your day. Or you might expect to be miserable and suddenly win the lottery. Figure 5.4 illustrates this fact well. The chart shows European consumer confidence and returns on European stocks over the last 10 years. When the stock market turned up, consumers felt better. When the stock market dropped, their moods soured. How consumers are feeling doesn't tell you much at all about where stocks are going.

Like the consumer confidence measure in Figure 5.4, there are a number of sentiment indicators investors follow closely. Many are surveys polling a portion of a targeted group to gauge whether people feel (a) very good, (b) decent, (c) downtrodden, or (d) outright lousy about the state of whatever it is they're trying to measure. Other sentiment indicators might not directly measure people's moods, but they are believed to reflect how people are feeling. For instance, investors are supposedly optimistic when money is flowing into equity mutual

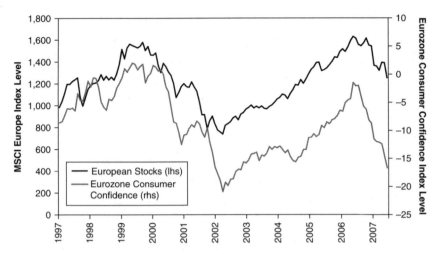

Figure 5.4   European Consumer Confidence and Stock Prices
Source: Thomson Datastream.

funds, and they're pessimistic when it's flowing into money market funds.

Sentiment indicators are most effective as investment tools when they're at extremes. And not in the way you might think. If investors are overly pessimistic, it's probably a good time to invest. In contrast, times when investors are euphoric are good times to be wary. Eighteenth-century banker Baron Philippe de Rothschild proclaimed the best time to buy is when there is "blood in the streets," referring to the bargains available during chaos and revolution. But the adage is just as applicable to investing in stocks. You'll probably have other things on your mind if you see a river of hemoglobin outside your window, but if you sense extreme investor pessimism about a particular country, sector, or region is undue, it's time to start looking for opportunities there.

The media is probably the most revealing sentiment barometer. Just look at the headlines and you can garner a pretty good idea about how people feel. In fact, it's often the media that sets the tone in the first place. It's hard not to feel bad about things if your favorite newspapers, magazines, websites, and TV shows are continually telling you things are bad. So if every investing "guru" you follow says real estate stocks will never recover, put a few on your watch list. And if you find yourself reading article after article claiming Chinese stocks won't drop for the next 50 years, think twice about putting too much money in China.

This doesn't mean a purely contrarian investment approach is the way to go. Contrarians doggedly do the opposite of what most investors believe will happen. Instead, look for areas where sentiment is detached from reality so you can take advantage of stock prices that don't reflect true fundamentals.

You could drive yourself crazy keeping track of every economic statistic, political situation, and sentiment indicator in the world. But global investing doesn't have to entail getting yourself committed. Most of the time, most of these indicators aren't telling you anything that will give you an advantage as a global investor. Remember, the stock market discounts widely known information, and the hoopla surrounding most of the information means it's known to just about everyone. But it can still be useful if others perceive it incorrectly— a more common occurrence than you might think. Try to interpret information differently than the crowds. Of course, this doesn't do you any good if you're interpreting it incorrectly, but don't assume others are getting it right.

One way to do this is to look for meaningless information others are blowing out of proportion. Remember the Y2K scare? In mid-1999, investors traded their stocks for gold bullion, canned food, and ammo in anticipation of global pandemonium caused by a few bits of errant computer code. The resulting drop in stock prices gave smart investors with eyes for manic, irrational behavior the chance to scoop up stocks at big discounts before markets finished the year with a bang.

STEP 3: STOCK PICKING

You know you want to own stocks, and you've decided what types of stocks to own. Hooray! You've already made the two most important investment decisions. Now it's time to peek into the world of bottom-up investing and pick some stocks. The fact many investors spend all their time focusing on stock picking, combined with the fact there are literally tens of thousands of stocks in the world, tells you there's a lot to it.

There are many different factors to consider, and they're going to be different for different kinds of stocks. I'm not going to do you the disservice of providing a one-size-fits-all, bottom-up investing kit. That would suggest there's a single correct approach to evaluating stocks. On the contrary, there are many different ways to go about choosing among individual firms. But it is a good idea to have a consistent process to maintain discipline. Once you get the hang of it, you'll undoubtedly refine your approach over time.

Here's a tool to get you started. This is called a *stock funnel* because it takes the enormous pool of global stocks and whittles it down to a more manageable few. The funnel in Figure 5.5 shows one way to turn the vast pool of global stocks into a portfolio.

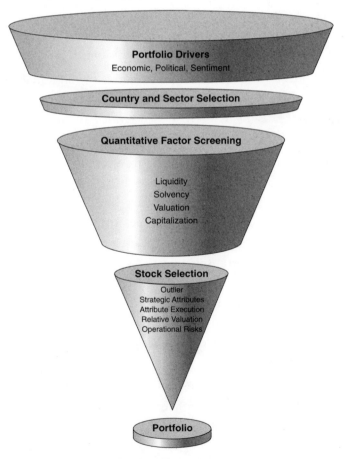

Figure 5.5   Stock-Picking Funnel

There are over 25,000 stocks in the world. Trying to do the most basic fundamental analysis on even a fraction of them is nearly impossible. Keep in mind you've already made some decisions that are going to help with the stock-picking process. Your top-down economic, political, and sentiment drivers will serve as your first screen. If you're looking for a large-cap foreign oil company, you've already taken most stocks off the table. But a series of quantitative screens will help you narrow the list further.

Quantitative Screens

Liquidity. Liquidity refers to the amount a stock trades. A liquidity screen ensures a stock regularly trades enough volume for you to buy and sell it at will. Some small or obscure stocks might not trade very often or in very large volume. So even for an individual investor, buying and selling shares can mean paying a big premium or selling at a discount.

Solvency. This is probably the most obvious of the bunch. It goes without saying you'd like the companies you own to stay in business. The solvency screen is intended to toss out companies on the brink of bankruptcy.

Valuation. Valuation refers to your sub-asset allocation decisions about growth and value. This is the *style* of stock you want to own. There is no hard and fast line delineating growth from value, so to a certain degree, the difference is in the eye of the investor. But there are some regularly agreed upon characteristics differentiating the two. Companies most considered *value* oriented tend to have lower valuation metrics such as price-to-earnings ratios, price-to-book ratios, and so on. They also tend to have higher dividend yields. *Growth* companies tend to reside at the other end of the spectrum by these measures.

Market capitalization. You've probably already decided whether you want to choose a large-, medium-, or small-sized stocks. A market cap screen weeds out the sizes of stock you're not interested in owning.

With the quantitative screens out of the way, you can get down to the fundamentals of the stocks you're considering. This is a more rigorous process.

Fundamental Screens

Outlier analysis. As a top-down investor, you want to own stocks that act like the countries and sectors they're intended to represent. A utility company whose stock acts more like a health-care company isn't giving you the exposure you want. Enron was this sort of company. Technically, Enron was an energy company, but it didn't act anything like other stocks in the sector. So top-down investors choosing Enron for their portfolios weren't getting the energy exposure they expected. The stocks you pick don't have to correlate perfectly with other stocks in their countries or sectors (as you know from Chapter 3, none will), but they shouldn't be wildly different, either.

Strategic attribute review. This is one of the most important fundamentals to consider. Look for companies with strategic attributes that give them advantages over their competitors. These can be things like a strong brand name, dominant market share, low production costs, or strong management—anything that positively differentiates a company from its peers. As you'll read in a moment, valuations are important, but attractive strategic attributes can be even more important over the long term.

Attribute execution analysis. Having a strategic attribute is nice, but it doesn't do a company much good if the company isn't taking advantage of it. Make sure companies are capitalizing on the strategic attributes you identified in the previous step.

For example, if a company is the low-cost producer in whatever it makes, but it doesn't have great profit margins or it's not picking up market share, the company isn't taking advantage of its strategic attribute.

Relative valuation analysis. Compare a firm's valuation to its peers to identify companies that seem overvalued or undervalued. If you're about to buy the most richly valued automaker in Germany, there might be a reason to think twice if the fundamentals don't justify the valuation. And undervalued companies could have hidden value investors aren't appreciating.

Operational risk assessment. Last, look for obvious red flags. If a company's founder owns half the shares, be aware she could decide to sell, putting downward pressure on the stock. A high business concentration with just a few customers could be problematic if one or several of the customers defect. Outstanding litigation could also be a risk, and so on.

The Global View

Now you're equipped with the tools to become a successful top-down global investor. The top-down approach isn't the only way to manage a global portfolio, but for most investors, it's the most effective way. Not only does top-down investing make the potentially daunting pool of global investment opportunities more manageable, it also provides an effective framework for controlling risk and capitalizing on economic, political, and sentiment drivers.

The next time your bottom-up investing friends are touting some new great stock, don't be afraid to ask about their country and sector exposure or which macroeconomic factors will impact the stock's performance. Their bewildered looks are part of the many rewards of top-down investing.

Four Steps to
Investing Success

Sometimes doing the right thing just feels wrong. Drinking the prescribed eight glasses of water a day may leave you feeling soggy. And we often opt for a candy bar when we should be reaching for a carrot stick. It's easy to get sidetracked from your long-term goals by the lure of short-term satisfaction. But there is no surer recipe for investing misfortune.

Navigating the global investing seas takes a steady hand and a steadier head. This chapter will provide you with four steps in a top-down strategy to help you stay the course. Don't think of these as rules. Think of them as guidelines, but essential guidelines. And you're not limited to just these four—you might find others to help you stay on track (e.g., don't run with scissors while investing, wait at least an hour after investing before you go for a swim). Tack on as many extra steps as you want, but these are your vital four:

1. Choose a benchmark.
2. Analyze the benchmark's components and assign expected risk and return.

3. Blend dissimilar investments to moderate risk relative to return.
4. Always remember you could be wrong, so don't stray from the first three steps.

STEP 1: CHOOSE A BENCHMARK

Step 1 involves a commonly used investing tool: a benchmark. Investing without a benchmark is like trying to circumnavigate the globe sans map. Without one, there's a good chance your portfolio gets hijacked by pirates. That's possibly a lesser risk, but you could, and likely will, hit an investment iceberg or two or end up in Madagascar when you were aiming for Lisbon. Very few investors utilize benchmarks, and many who do don't get the full benefit because they ignore their most important function.

What the Heck Is a Benchmark?

First: What exactly is a benchmark? A benchmark is just an index tracking whatever asset you're investing in. There are real estate indexes tracking real estate prices, bond indexes tracking bond prices, commodity indexes tracking commodity prices—you get the picture.

Naturally, a stock index is an appropriate benchmark for stock investors. But as discussed in Chapter 4, there are many different types of stocks, so there are also many different types of stock indexes. You'll find indexes tracking large stocks, small stocks, domestic stocks, foreign stocks, oil stocks, retail stocks—you name it, there's a good chance there's an index tracking it. Virtually any of these could be used as benchmarks. But just as following the wrong map could mean ending up in Sri Lanka instead of Shreveport, choosing an inappropriate benchmark can throw your portfolio way off course.

A Benchmark Is a Many-Splendored Thing

To pick the right benchmark, you must first know how a benchmark is used. A benchmark serves two main functions for top-down investors.

It's a Yardstick.   The first function is simple—a benchmark acts as a yardstick to measure portfolio performance. Too many investors focus on absolute performance. Did my investment portfolio go up or down, and by how much? But absolute returns don't tell the whole story. Is a 20 percent return in any given year good? It depends on your benchmark. Few investors would be disappointed by a 20 percent return, but what if the benchmark was up 40 percent? How would you feel about a 20 percent return if you had all your money invested in China in 2007? That year, China's Shanghai A Index was up over 110 percent (in US dollars)! A 20 percent return seems awfully meager by comparison. But a 20 percent return for an investor with all her money in Ireland in 2007 would make her dance a jig. Irish markets actually fell by 20 percent for US investors that year. In order to properly assess your portfolio's performance, you must compare it to an appropriate benchmark.

Scaling your returns properly is a key benchmark function, but a benchmark is arguably more important in its next role.

It's a Roadmap.   Your benchmark also serves as a guide when building your global investment portfolio. As explained in Chapter 5, finding attractive stocks is an important step in the investment process, but there are far more important decisions to make— namely, how much do you want to invest in each country, sector, or industry?

Before making these decisions, check your benchmark. Analyze its components to see how it's constructed. Putting 50 percent of your portfolio in Utilities might seem like a good idea, particularly if you really like Utilities. But if Utilities comprise just 5 percent of your benchmark, you're taking an enormous risk—probably way more than you think. Once you know your benchmark inside and out, you move on to Step 2 and assign expected risk and return to each component. Then you can decide how much more or less of each type of stock (growth, value, small, large, Energy, Health Care, etc.) you want to include in your portfolio. But first, you must know what to look for in a benchmark.

Indexes Aren't Created Equal

How you use a benchmark doesn't matter much if you've got the wrong benchmark. Choosing an appropriate index as a benchmark is essential to proper portfolio construction and evaluation, so just any index won't do.

There are literally hundreds of thousands of indexes tracking different kinds of stocks in different countries and sectors throughout the world. An inappropriate or poorly constructed benchmark can prevent you from making good investment decisions, adequately managing risk, and properly measuring your portfolio's performance. Here are some of the characteristics differentiating good benchmarks from bad.

Weight Watchers.   Of the many, many thousands of indexes, most are either *price weighted* or *capitalization weighted*. (The latter are also known as *market-value weighted* indexes.) You'll find a few other variants out there. Equal-weighted indexes assign the same weight to every stock. And fundamentally weighted indexes use things like dividend yields and earnings-per-share to affix weights. But these are much less common. It's most important to distinguish between price- and capitalization-weighted indexes.

In a price-weighted index, the price of a stock determines how much influence that stock has on the index. Here's how it works: Imagine you have an index consisting of stocks in two firms. Small Cap Co. trades at $100 per share and has a market capitalization of $1 billion. Big Cap Inc. trades at just $1 per share, but it has a market capitalization of $100 billion. Big Cap Inc. is clearly a much larger firm. But in a price-weighted index, Small Cap Co. with the $100 stock price would have about *100 times* the impact of the much larger Big Cap Inc.

Imagine a particularly volatile day in which shares of Small Cap Co. shot up 10 percent but Big Cap Inc. slumped 20 percent. Table 6.1 shows how the return on our price-weighted index would be calculated.

Table 6.1   Calculating Returns for a Price-Weighted Index

Company	Share Price	Weight in the Index		% Change		Impact
Small Cap Co.	$100	0.99	×	+10%	=	+9.9%
Big Cap Inc.	$1	0.01	×	−20%	=	−0.2%
Sum the impacts to get the return for the index						+9.7%

The index rose 9.7 percent even though the combined market value of the two stocks fell by almost $20 billion! Seem perplexing? It should. The price of a stock is completely arbitrary. It doesn't tell you how much money is invested in a company. It doesn't tell you how the stock has performed. It doesn't tell you anything about anything except how much it costs to buy a single share. Price-weighted indexes don't make much sense from an investing standpoint because they don't reflect how money is actually invested.

Not so with capitalization-weighted indexes. In a capitalization-weighted index, the total market capitalization of a company determines its weight. Using the same two stocks from above, Big Cap Inc. would have 100 times the impact of Small Cap Co. in a capitalization-weighted index. Using the same price changes as above, Table 6.2 shows how the return on our capitalization-weighted index is calculated.

The capitalization-weighted index fell by the same amount as the decline in the combined market capitalization of the two stocks. Capitalization-weighted indexes make better benchmarks because they reflect reality—how money is actually invested.

Table 6.2   Calculating Returns for a Market Capitalization–Weighted Index

Company	Market Cap	Weight in the Index		% Change		Impact
Small Cap Co.	$1 billion	0.01	×	+10%	=	+0.10%
Big Cap Inc.	$100 billion	0.99	×	−20%	=	−19.8%
Sum the impacts to get the return for the index						−19.7%

Big 'Ol Berkshire

$100,000 will buy a lot of things. It'll get you an arm full of Rolexes, a closet full of Jimmy Choo shoes, or buckets of Beluga caviar. But it wont even get you a single share of Berkshire Hathaway Inc. Berkshire has been one of the best performing stocks in the US over the last few decades, but that's not the reason its shares have reached such stratospheric levels. Firms like Microsoft and Oracle have outpaced Berkshire over the last 20 years, but a share of either of those companies will cost you about 99.98 percent less than a share of Berkshire.

The main reason for Berkshire's ultra-high price isn't performance, but the fact Berkshire has never split its stock. Firms will occasionally split shares to make the price more attractive to investors. Stock splits don't change the value of a company; they simply lower the share price and increase the number of shares outstanding by a corresponding amount. (The opposite happens in a reverse split.) If you owned one share of a stock with a $200 stock price, after a 2:1 stock split, you'd own two shares worth $100 each.

Why doesn't Berkshire split its stock? Warren Buffet and the folks at Berkshire believe splitting the stock would lead to higher transaction costs (more shares usually means more commissions for brokers) and attract investors more concerned about short-run gains than the long-run success of the company. This rhetorical question posed by Mr. Buffet himself sums up the company's stance on the issue:

> Could we really improve our shareholder group by trading some of our present clear-thinking members for impressionable new ones who, preferring paper to value, feel wealthier with nine $10 bills than with one $100 bill?

Berkshire not only has a big stock price, it's also a big company. So it will have a significant impact on either a price- or capitalization-weighted index. But its effect on the former would be out of this world.

Source: Thomson Datastream; 1983 Berkshire Hathaway Chairman's Letter.

The Dodgy Dow. Two of the best-known stock indexes in the world, especially for US investors, are the Dow Jones Industrial Average and the S&P 500 Index. Both are intended to track US stock performance, but the Dow is price weighted whereas the S&P 500 is capitalization weighted.

It's probably no coincidence the Dow is the older of the two. The Dow was created in 1896. At the time, it was a lot easier to calculate the performance of a price-weighted index than a capitalization-weighted one. Without the benefit of calculators or computers, changes in the index value had to be figured by hand. In a price-weighted index, only one input is needed—the stock price. However, calculating the performance of a capitalization-weighted index meant getting timely information on the number of shares outstanding in a company as well.

Needless to say, reporting standards weren't as robust in the nineteenth century as they are today, so getting accurate information to calculate the performance of a capitalization-weighted index was more difficult. Even the keeper of the Dow, Dow Jones & Company, weights most of its newer indexes by capitalization. But the storied Dow has kept its price-weighted structure.

Alas, the Dow isn't alone with its faults. Japan's popular Nikkei 225 is also price weighted. Fortunately, most indexes these days tend to be capitalization weighted, like Germany's DAX 30, Hong Kong's Hang Seng, Japan's Topix, France's CAC 40, and UK's FTSE All-Share.

Float.   Now, a wrinkle: These days, most capitalization-weighted indexes include a *float* adjustment. Each firm's weight in a capitalization-weighted, float-adjusted index is determined by the value of the shares that are actually available to trade, not the total value of the company. For some companies, the difference is minimal. But for others, it's quite meaningful.

Definition

Float

A firm's market capitalization is calculated by multiplying the share price by the number of shares outstanding. But not all these shares are available to trade. Every firm has some shares tied up with investors who can't sell them. Why? It usually depends on

(Continued)

the type of shareholders and the relationship with the firm whose shares they own. Company executives, corporations, governments, and controlling shareholders can't just lob a call to their brokers and place sell orders. Their shares are usually locked up, sometimes for years. And when they are able to sell, there are additional regulatory hoops to jump through.

If you subtract these locked-up shares from all the shares outstanding, you get the float. Float-adjusted indexes use this to figure companies' weights rather than the total shares outstanding. So instead of multiplying the share price by the shares outstanding, they multiply the share price by the float to get the float-adjusted market capitalization.

As said previously, the S&P 500 is more useful than the Dow for tracking US stocks because the S&P 500 is capitalization weighted. But it's also float adjusted, so firms like Wal-Mart actually have a smaller weight in the index than their market capitalization seems to call for.

In 2007, Wal-Mart was the eighth-largest US firm by market capitalization. But it was only the 26th-largest weight in the S&P 500,[1] behind firms like Coca-Cola and Hewlett-Packard, which were significantly smaller but have larger portions of their shares available to trade. That's because a huge chunk of Wal-Mart's shares are held by members of founder Sam Walton's family, and they can't just sell shares whenever they'd like.

More Is More.   The weighting structure isn't the only difference among stock indexes. There frequently are dramatic differences in the number of stocks included in each. Technically, an index could include just one stock if its focus were narrow enough. An index tracking the performance of firms selling suntan lotion in Antarctica isn't likely to have many stocks to choose from. But broader indexes should contain a sufficient number of stocks to reflect the entire market and also minimize the impact of stock-specific issues.

With only 30 constituents, the Dow falls short once again. So do Germany's Deutscher Aktien Index 30 (thankfully, better known as the DAX 30) and France's Cotation Assistée en Continu (aka the CAC 40). With 500 constituents, the S&P 500 does a pretty good job of representing US stocks, but there are broader US indexes still. The Russell 3000 Index contains 3,000 US stocks (rather obviously). But don't be fooled by the Dow Jones Wilshire 5000 Index. It contains every stock in the US with "readily available price data"—over 6,500 in total! Japan's Tokyo Stock Price Index (the Topix) has over 1,700 members. The UK's Financial Times Stock Exchange All-Share Index (FTSE All-Share) contains about 660. These broader indexes do a better job reflecting the specific markets they represent. For more, Table 6.3 shows the number of stocks comprising a number of stock indexes from around the world.

Table 6.3   Index Constituents

Index	Country	Number of Constituents
S&P 500	US	500
S&P/ASX All Ordinaries	Australia	500
S&P/TSX	Canada	253
Nikkei 225	Japan	225
Hang Seng	Hong Kong	43
CAC 40	France	40
DAX 30	Germany	30
Dow 30	US	30
Swiss Market	Switzerland	20
MSCI World	Global	~1,900
MSCI All Country World	Global	~2,900
Dow-Wilshire Developed Market	Global	~11,000
Dow-Wilshire Global Total Market	Global	~13,000
FTSE Developed All Cap	Global	~6,200
FTSE Global Equity Series All Cap	Global	~8,000
S&P/Citigroup World Broad Market	Global	~8,800
S&P/Citigroup Global Broad Market	Global	~11,200

Source: Bloomberg Finance L.P.

Global Indexes

You've probably run across many of the indexes at the top of Table 6.3. These are some of the world's most commonly known, widely quoted indexes. Many are broad and capitalization weighted, but these are just the basic requirements for an index to be considered as a suitable benchmark. Not every index with these characteristics makes the grade when it comes to global investing. After all, choosing an index tracking just small stocks doesn't make sense unless you're building a portfolio of small stocks. And you wouldn't choose an index of bank stocks unless you're focusing on that specific industry. Similarly, the most appropriate benchmark for a global portfolio is an index reflecting the performance of global equity markets.

Many of the indexes listed in Table 6.3 represent individual countries. A global investor needs a benchmark not confined by borders—representing stocks throughout the world. I snuck a few of these in at the bottom of the table. You might not be as familiar with them, but you will be before this chapter is through.

Engineering an Index

There are several firms whose primary (or at least, major) function is creating and maintaining indexes—engineering indexes tracking companies in just about every country and every industry possible. At first blush, this might not seem like a fruitful business endeavor. After all, you can get free data for most indexes on the Internet or in the newspaper. But the index business is more profitable than you might think. Why? Because people in the financial services industry, like me, want to delve into index nitty-gritty. We pore over individual index members. We long for historical data. We want returns calculated in every currency—from the Albanian lek to the Zambian kwacha. We've discovered innumerable ways to obsess over every minutia. Don't worry. You needn't torment yourself to the same degree to build a perfectly fine global portfolio. But you must know some of the details about your chosen benchmark.

Index Note

All the indexes highlighted through the end of this chapter are capitalization weighted and float adjusted, but they use different methodologies. Chapter 4 outlined the two most common classification systems for grouping companies by primary business line—the Global Industry Classification Standard (GICS) and the Industry Classification Benchmark (ICB). The index producers highlighted here use one of these two. In fact, they developed them.

Recall, GICS and ICB take different approaches to differentiating between "developed" and "emerging" markets. Additionally, the indexes contain vastly different numbers of stocks. More stocks doesn't necessarily make one better than another as long as they're all sufficiently diverse. These indexes all contain an adequate number of stocks to accurately reflect global markets, and that's what's important.

Here's a look at a few of the companies in the index business and some of the indexes they've created that will serve the global investor well.

MSCI.   MSCI Inc. (aka MSCI Barra) is one such company. MSCI stands for Morgan Stanley Capital International. The first of the MSCI indexes was created by Capital International Group before the company was acquired by Morgan Stanley in 1985. MSCI Inc. has since been spun off from Morgan Stanley as an independent, publicly traded company.

MSCI has created some of the most commonly used sector, country, regional, and global indexes. MSCI, along with Standard & Poor's, also developed the GICS classification methodology, so MSCI indexes utilize this standard. In total, MSCI maintains over 100,000 indexes (you read that correctly—100,000!).[2] A few of these are of particular use to US investors looking to build global portfolios.

The *MSCI EAFE Index* (EAFE for short) tracks stocks in developed markets outside North America. EAFE stands for Europe, Australasia (a clever fusion of Australia and Asia), and Far East. It's currently composed of about 1,300 stocks from 21 different countries.[3] The EAFE notably excludes Canadian companies, but despite shunning our neighbors to the north, the EAFE serves as a good bellwether for foreign stock performance. So if you're sitting on a portfolio of US stocks and looking to expand globally, the EAFE will get you started.

The EAFE might get you going down the path of global investing, but it's not truly global. Recall, North American equity markets are the largest of any region, so excluding North America leaves out a big piece of the global pie. The MSCI World Index goes a step further. It's essentially the EAFE Index with the US and Canada thrown in. It currently includes over 1,900 stocks from 23 countries.[4]

Twenty-three countries might seem like broad global exposure, and it is, but the MSCI World Index isn't all-inclusive. It excludes stocks from some important markets. China, India, Brazil, Russia—these and other emerging markets aren't represented in the MSCI World. Why? As you'll find out in the next chapter, emerging markets make up a small portion of global stock markets. And many emerging markets have only opened their doors to foreign investors over the last decade or so. But the global landscape is changing, and there's no doubt emerging markets are becoming more important. Therefore, it's increasingly necessary to include some emerging-market exposure in a global portfolio. The MSCI All Country World Index (MSCI ACWI, or just ACWI for us lazy folks) does just that. It's the MSCI World Index plus emerging markets. There are almost 2,900 stocks in the ACWI representing 48 countries.

Dow-Wilshire.   MSCI isn't the only player in the global index game. Dow Jones manages many prominent indexes as well. The Dow Jones Industrial Average is the oldest and best known, but it is just one of over 130,000 indexes Dow Jones manages. In 2004, Dow Jones partnered with Wilshire Associates to create a global index series.[5] Like the MSCI indexes, these are sliced and diced into indexes tracking just about every country, region, and industry imaginable. But there are a few meaningful differences between the MSCI and Dow Jones

Wilshire indexes. Dow Jones uses the ICB system to classify companies instead of GICS. And whereas MSCI categorizes 23 countries as "developed," Dow Jones includes these and South Korea, Taiwan, Israel, Cyprus, and Iceland in the developed category for a total of 28.

For global investors, the jewels of the Dow Jones Wilshire Global Indexes are the Dow Jones Wilshire Developed Market Index and the Dow Jones Wilshire Global Total Market Index. Like the MSCI World Index, the Dow Jones Wilshire Developed Market Index excludes countries Dow Jones considers emerging. Still, this index includes almost 11,000 stocks with a combined market capitalization of almost $44 trillion.[6]

Similar to the MSCI ACWI Index, the Dow Jones Wilshire Global Total Market Index includes both developed and emerging markets—close to 13,000 stocks from 58 countries, representing a total market capitalization of over $50 trillion!

FTSE. FTSE Group (say it with me, "footsie") is a joint collaboration between the *Financial Times* and the London Stock Exchange, managing over 100,000 indexes. The FTSE Developed All Cap Index and the FTSE Global Equity Series All Cap Index are FTSE's broadest global indexes. Like Dow Jones, FTSE uses the ICB classification system, which is not surprising, considering the companies developed this classification system together.

Similar to MSCI and Dow Jones, FTSE categorizes countries as either "developed" or "emerging." The FTSE Developed All Cap Index includes stocks from the 24 countries FTSE considers developed. But unlike MSCI and Dow Jones, FTSE divides emerging countries into "advanced emerging" and "secondary emerging" depending on the level of development. The FTSE Global Equity Series All Cap Index includes stocks from both. In all, the FTSE Global Equity Series All Cap Index contains over 8,000 stocks from 48 countries.

S&P. Last, there's Standard & Poor's, better known as S&P. Many think of S&P as a credit rating agency, but the company manages many indexes as well. In fact, there's more than $5 trillion benchmarked to S&P indexes, thanks largely to the prominent role of the S&P 500 in the US.[7]

S&P's global indexes include the S&P/Citigroup World Broad Market Index, which covers developed markets only, and the S&P/ Citigroup Global Broad Market Index, which includes both developed and emerging markets. The latter includes over 9,000 stocks from 52 countries.

Which index should you choose as your benchmark? Frankly, it doesn't matter much. Each of these indexes has the right characteristics. There are some differences in the way they're constructed and managed, but they're similar enough that they should have nearly identical risk and return characteristics over time. My advice is to go with the broader indexes. They'll give you a little more diversification and a few more investment options. But if you'd prefer to stick to developed markets, you won't do materially worse with an index that eschews developing countries.

The next step in the top-down process will provide some additional insights into the composition of global indexes. But you'll be well-served by taking a look at each firm's website. If you think one gives you easier access to the data you need than the others, choose that one. It's that easy. Remember, the benchmark is just a starting point, but an essential one. From there you can strive to outperform global equity markets using the tools we provide in the next steps.

STEP 2: ANALYZE THE BENCHMARK'S COMPONENTS AND ASSIGN EXPECTED RISK AND RETURN

Step 1 was like a first date with your benchmark. You chitchatted, didn't talk about yourself too much, and waited just long enough to call again so as to not seem desperate. Now you're done with the pleasantries. It's time to really get to know your benchmark.

Step 2 involves taking a closer look at the aforementioned indexes to see how they're built. Once you know their compositions, you can assess each piece of your benchmark individually. Then you can utilize the top-down methods from the previous chapter to determine which pieces have the best risk and return characteristics—thereby deserving extra attention—and which pieces don't get a second date.

We'll start with one of the developed markets indexes. Table 6.4 shows the country breakdown for the MSCI World Index. As mentioned, the different index providers use different methodologies, so a similar breakdown of the other developed market indexes will look slightly different. But all are out to accomplish about the same thing

Table 6.4   MSCI World Country Breakdown

Country	Weight
US	47.1%
UK	10.8%
Japan	9.7%
France	5.2%
Germany	4.6%
Canada	4.1%
Switzerland	3.3%
Australia	3.2%
Spain	2.1%
Italy	1.9%
Netherlands	1.4%
Hong Kong	1.2%
Sweden	1.1%
Finland	0.9%
Belgium	0.6%
Singapore	0.5%
Norway	0.5%
Denmark	0.5%
Greece	0.4%
Ireland	0.3%
Austria	0.3%
Portugal	0.2%
New Zealand	0.1%

Source: Thomson Datastream; MSCI Inc.[8]

(to reflect the make-up of global equity markets), so the differences aren't huge. The main most distinguishing characteristic will be the countries included. Remember, each index provider classifies developed and emerging countries differently, so countries such as South Korea will show up in Dow, FTSE, and S&P developed indexes but not MSCI's.

Just as important as the country breakdown is the composition by business type, which you'll find in Table 6.5. Remember, MSCI and S&P use the GICS classification system whereas Dow and FTSE use ICB, so the categories won't match up exactly, but they'll be close.

Table 6.5   MSCI World Sector Breakdown

Sector	Weight
Financials	22.4%
Industrials	11.2%
Energy	10.9%
Information Technology	11.0%
Consumer Discretionary	9.8%
Consumer Staples	8.8%
Health Care	8.7%
Materials	7.1%
Utilities	4.7%
Telecommunication Services	4.9%

Source: Thomson Datastream; MSCI Inc., as of December 31, 2007.[9]

Table 6.6 shows the country breakdown of the MSCI ACWI. The weights of the emerging countries are highlighted, and the combined weight of the emerging countries is listed below. Even though emerging countries get a lot of press these days for being the hottest up-and-coming markets, developed countries still make up the lion's share of global indexes.

Table 6.7 includes the sector breakdown of the MSCI ACWI. Note the sector weights aren't much different than the developed market index. The Materials and Energy came up a little because emerging countries tend to have higher weights in these areas. And Health

Table 6.6   MSCI ACWI Country Breakdown

Country	Weight	Country	Weight
US	41.8%	Norway	0.5%
UK	9.6%	Denmark	0.4%
Japan	8.6%	Greece	0.3%
France	4.6%	Malaysia	0.3%
Germany	4.1%	Ireland	0.3%
Canada	3.7%	Austria	0.2%
Switzerland	2.9%	Israel	0.2%
Australia	2.8%	Turkey	0.2%
Spain	1.9%	Poland	0.2%
China	1.8%	Indonesia	0.2%
Italy	1.7%	Portugal	0.2%
South Korea	1.6%	Thailand	0.2%
Brazil	1.5%	Chile	0.1%
Netherlands	1.2%	Egypt	0.1%
Russia	1.1%	Hungary	0.1%
Taiwan	1.1%	Czech Republic	0.1%
Hong Kong	1.1%	Peru	0.1%
Sweden	1.0%	Philippines	0.1%
India	0.9%	New Zealand	0.1%
Finland	0.8%	Argentina	0.1%
South Africa	0.8%	Colombia	0.0%
Belgium	0.5%	Morocco	0.0%
Mexico	0.5%	Pakistan	0.0%
Singapore	0.5%	Jordan	0.0%
Total Emerging Market Weight			**11.3%**

Source: Thomson Datastream; MSCI Inc.[10]

Care and Consumer Discretionary dropped down. But the relatively small weight of emerging markets in general means the sector/industry weights don't change much.

When it comes to investing in most countries, you can't be too granular. Canada is basically Canada, Portugal is basically Portugal, and Chile is basically Chile. There might be some unique features to different areas of a country. If real estate is booming in Sydney but

Table 6.7 MSCI ACWI Sector Breakdown

Sector	Weight
Financials	22.5%
Energy	11.7%
Industrials	11.2%
Information Technology	10.9%
Consumer Discretionary	9.2%
Consumer Staples	8.3%
Materials	8.0%
Health Care	7.9%
Telecommunication Services	5.6%
Utilities	4.6%

Source: Thomson Datastream; MSCI Inc.[11]

not in Perth, banks doing more mortgage lending on Australia's east coast might fare better. But most stocks in a country will share the same currency, tax code, trade restrictions, and so on.

But remember, sectors in GICS and industries in ICB are just the highest levels of classification. Companies in these broad categories often aren't affected by the same drivers. An insurance stock isn't necessarily going to act like a bank stock just because they're both Financials. And a mining stock won't act like a paper stock just because they're both Materials companies. So your analysis of the types of stocks you invest in shouldn't stop at the highest classification level.

So, how to use this information? It depends on the type of investor you are. As mentioned in Chapter 1, you can be either passive or active.

Passive

If it seems like there are a lot of decisions associated with global investing, you might be relieved to read you can get the benefits of a global portfolio without making many decisions at all. This is the *passive* approach. Being passive isn't anything to be ashamed of. It doesn't make you any less of an investor. There are plenty of ladder-climbing, risk-taking, base-jumping, shark-wrestling, alpha males (and females) out there who prefer passive over active.

The passive approach to global investing simply means making your portfolio look as much like your global benchmark as possible. A passive investor choosing the MSCI World Index as his benchmark would want 10.9 percent of his portfolio in Energy stocks, 8.8 percent in Consumer Staples stocks, and 11.2 percent in Industrials (see Table 6.5 for these). He'd also have 5.2 percent invested in France, 1.4 percent in the Netherlands, and 0.5 percent in Denmark (see Table 6.6)—or as close to these weights as possible. In top-down parlance, this is known as being *neutral weight* to these countries and sectors. The goal here is to match the performance of the benchmark by being benchmark-like.

Definition

Overweight, Underweight, and Neutral Weight

For each country, sector, industry, and style, top-down global investors can choose to be overweight, underweight, or neutral weight. Being *overweight* means owning more of a particular class of stock than is present in a benchmark. Being *underweight* means owning relatively less than the benchmark. And a *neutral weight* is when the portfolio holds the same proportion as the benchmark in a particular area. Passive investors try to maintain neutral weights to all types of stocks. Active investors maintain overweight positions in areas they expect to do relatively well and underweight positions in areas they expect to do relatively poorly.

Passive portfolios require little maintenance. Benchmarks are reshuffled occasionally so passive portfolios will have to be too, but the necessary adjustments are minimal. This might sound like an ideal approach to global investing, but there are drawbacks. Passive investors usually do worse than—or *lag*—their benchmarks, thanks to the fees associated with investing. But sometimes they get lucky. Managers of passive portfolios might not own all the stocks in their benchmarks. A manager benchmarked against the MSCI World Index probably won't buy all of the roughly 1,900 index constituents.

Instead, she'll buy a smaller group of stocks she thinks will match the performance of the index. Since it's slightly different than the benchmark, the portfolio might outperform at times even though that's not the goal.

And passive investors often use mutual or exchange-traded funds rather than individual stocks, which, as explained in the next chapter, is usually less tax efficient. But if you prefer to spend your time skydiving rather than investing, a passive approach might work for you.

Active

Active investors take a different approach. They try to outperform their chosen benchmarks by making investment decisions that differentiate their portfolios from their benchmarks. Active investors believing technology stocks will outperform the overall market will own a higher percentage of technology stocks than is in their benchmarks. In other words, they'll be *overweight* technology. Those believing technology stocks will do worse than the overall market will be *underweight* technology.

Inevitably, active investors will do better than their benchmarks some years. But they'll also get some decisions wrong and do worse than their benchmarks other years. How active investors do relative to their benchmarks (the best way to measure performance) depends on the quality of their decision making. But getting a few decisions wrong doesn't have to sink your portfolio entirely if you follow Steps 3 and 4. (Incidentally, Chapter 7 will outline investment options for both passive and active investors.)

STEP 3: BLEND DISSIMILAR INVESTMENTS TO MODERATE RISK RELATIVE TO RETURN

Many investors think their goal should be to make as much money as possible—they want to *maximize returns*. Think again. It's not that I dislike money. On the contrary, I'd like to sip champagne from the deck of an obnoxiously large yacht as much as the next person. But constantly trying to maximize returns usually means taking excessive risks, and that can turn your Dom Pérignon into Pabst Blue Ribbon in a hurry. Instead of trying to maximize your returns, active investors should try to consistently outperform their benchmarks—but not by a ton. As covered in Step 2, active investors will want to own relatively more of the types of stocks they expect to do well, but they shouldn't ignore the others entirely. Think of these as *core* and *counter* strategies. If your core strategy falls flat, your counter strategy just might save the day. The performance of health care and technology stocks in 2000, as seen in Figure 6.1, provides an example.

After a raging bull market for technology firms in the late 1990s, tech cratered in 2000. The tech-heavy NASDAQ Index lost over 40 percent that year—a serious setback if you'd bet the farm there. Investors also owning some health-care stocks as a counter strategy, even if they believed tech was going to continue its stratospheric rise, fared much better. Incorporate a counter strategy for when things don't go as planned. As covered in Chapter 3, all major categories of stocks get you to the same place in the long run, so there's no need to make a huge bet in any single area.

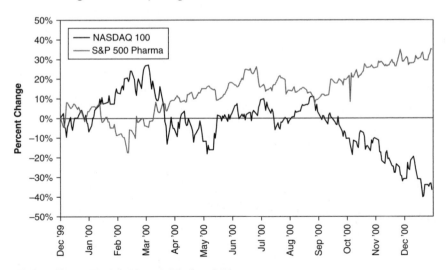

Figure 6.1   Drugs Versus Tech 2000

Source: Thomson Datastream; MSCI Inc.[12]

Building both core and counter strategies into your portfolio does more than just hedge your bets. Remember all that zigging and zagging from Chapter 3? A quick refresher: Mixing investments that move differently in the short term, but about the same in the long term, reduces the volatility of a portfolio without sacrificing long-term returns. Think of your core portfolio holdings as the ziggers and the counter strategy holdings as the zaggers. Or the other way around. It doesn't matter just as long as you've got some of each.

This is just the first step in portfolio risk management. The theme of blending dissimilar assets to moderate risk is an important one, but it's not as simple as finding a few investments you don't like to go along with the ones you do. Investment risk management is sophisticated business. So much so, it's beyond the scope of this book. A thorough job of risk analysis means analyzing betas, correlations, volatility, variance, and a multitude of other factors. But risk control and diversification are fundamental investing considerations, so always keep risk in mind when designing your portfolio.

STEP 4: ALWAYS REMEMBER YOU COULD BE WRONG, SO DON'T STRAY FROM THE FIRST THREE STEPS

Always remember: You can and will be wrong. This might seem like the easiest of the four steps to follow, but for many, staying disciplined can be difficult. Call it hubris, chutzpah, audacity, or a blatant disregard for reason. Many people are drawn toward reckless decisions like moths to a flame.

Why do we make these careless decisions so often? That's a question behavioralists will ponder until the end of time. You could blame your caveman ancestors for getting your brain hardwired for this sort of tomfoolery. For them, the dangerous task of bagging a woolly mammoth meant feeding the clan for a month. Now we love the grand slam, the hole-in-one, the 90-yard touchdown pass, and the half-court jump shot at the buzzer. In investing, that translates to going for the fast money. Unfortunately, too often the only thing *fast* about it is how the money leaves your portfolio.

From an investing standpoint, knowing why people make foolish decisions is much less important than recognizing we do make them. Controlling your instincts to stray from your long-term plan can be the most challenging part of investing.

The Global View

As just about any athlete will tell you these days, it's not easy to follow the rules (baseball steroids scandal, anyone?). But for investors, ignoring the steps laid out in this chapter can result in consequences more dire than getting benched or traded to another team: It can mean failing to meet your long-term investment objectives.

Remember, your benchmark is your starting point. Refer to it frequently, especially when contemplating making changes to your portfolio. The more you veer from your benchmark, the more risk you're taking. Taking some risk is part and parcel of investing, but understanding those risks separates wise from foolish investors.

I'm Convinced . . .
Now Tell Me How

None of what you've read about global investing means much if you don't know how to actually do it. Global investment options aren't limitless, but there are enough to throw even the most seasoned investor for a loop. Fortunately, these fall into a few main categories.

This chapter covers the four investment options most useful to global investors: mutual funds, exchange-traded funds (ETFs), depository receipts, and plain old ordinary shares. A good understanding of these enables just about anyone to build a global portfolio fit for a queen, prime minister, president, czar, or emperor.

WHO DOESN'T WANT MORE TIME AND MONEY?

If there are two things most people wish they had more of, it's time and money. Sure, people want happiness, but most will say they need at least a little time and money to be truly happy. Good health is also a priority, but time and money are important to health, too. It turns out time and money are also crucial when deciding how to invest globally.

Time on Your Side

Building a global portfolio can be straightforward or it can be extremely intricate. And the levels of complexity cover just about every degree of difficulty in between. The amount of time you can or want to commit to managing your portfolio will help determine your approach. After all, there are many different options for building a global portfolio, but there are even more ways to spend your time.

Global investing takes some time. There's no way around it. Even if you hire someone to do it for you, you've got to go through the process of choosing that person or people and pay attention to how your portfolio is doing. But the simplest approaches won't keep you off the golf course too long. As you'll read later in this chapter, there are a number of global mutual funds and exchange-traded funds available that provide access to equity markets around the world. If your portfolio is large enough to hire a professional money manager to manage a portfolio of individual stocks, all the better. An occasional check of your portfolio aside, you can commence with cocktail hour.

In contrast, building and monitoring your own portfolio of individual stocks can be time-consuming. Just choosing the stocks is a big undertaking, especially for an individual investor. But the job doesn't end there. There are innumerable press releases, earnings announcements, valuation metrics, and other things to rummage through regularly. And don't forget the top-down lessons. There are also economic, political, and sentiment drivers to monitor to make sure your sub-asset allocations are up to par.

If kicking back with a margarita isn't your thing, but you don't want to spend sleepless nights researching stocks either, you'll be happy to know there's fertile middle ground. Global investors needn't pore over every investment option. Choose a few areas in which you're interested or have some expertise and focus your efforts there. You can take a more casual approach to the rest of your portfolio. If you've worked in the oil business all your life and think you know a thing or two about oil firms, you can pick individual stocks in the industry and use mutual funds or ETFs for the rest. If you've done a lot of business in Europe during your career and are familiar with firms there, you might consider confining specific investment decisions to that region and outsourcing your exposure elsewhere. But don't get so caught up in your favorites that you forget about overall portfolio composition. Just because you're a self-proclaimed techie doesn't mean your portfolio should be massively overweight in technology stocks. Remember, one of the main functions of your benchmark is to provide risk control. Ignore it at your peril.

Size Matters

Possibly the most important factor determining the best way to build a global portfolio is size. Whether you choose individual stocks or lean on mutual funds and ETFs to gain exposure to global markets should depend largely on how much money you plan to invest. Generally, the bigger the portfolio, the more you should rely on individual stocks. There are enough advantages to holding stocks that it should be the favored approach for virtually all investors (regardless of portfolio size) if not for one nasty little consideration—transaction costs.

Why is it generally better to hold individual stocks? For one thing, owning stocks can be tax efficient. At any given time, a well-diversified portfolio will likely hold some stocks that have done well and some that have done poorly. That's ok. There's no need to decry those underperforming investments. As long as your overall portfolio is performing well, don't fret holding a few laggards. If all your stocks were moving up or down together, you'd be missing out on the volatility-reducing benefits of diversification outlined in Chapter 3. So if you've realized some capital gains in a taxable account by selling some winners during the year, you can frequently offset those gains and reduce your tax bill by selling some losers before the year ends. Additionally, even though stock selection doesn't have the biggest impact on your portfolio's performance, there's enough value to be added through stock selection to make it worthwhile.

However, buying individual stocks requires paying transaction fees. The bigger the portfolio, the less relative impact these costs have. But for smaller portfolios, transaction costs can be a high hurdle.

Definition

Bid-Ask Spread

If you go to a garage sale and spy a velvet Elvis you can't live without, the price you pay for your art is the same price the seller receives. But when you buy or sell most financial assets (stocks, ETFs, currencies, derivatives, etc.), the price one investor pays is usually more than another investor collects. The different prices are known as the *bid* and the *ask*.

The so-called *bid-ask spread* represents a transaction cost that often goes unnoticed. The stock price you watch scrolling across your TV screen is the price at which the last trade occurred. It gives you a good idea about where a stock is trading, but it doesn't reveal at what price you can actually buy or sell. That scrolling price doesn't tell you if the last transaction took place at the bid price, the ask price, or somewhere in between. Quite often, shares don't trade right at the bid or the ask. Sellers might be willing to lower their prices a little to find a buyer and buyers might pay a tad more to land their desired stock.

The difference between the bid and the ask is usually pretty small for the most liquid stocks because a lot of people are buying and selling shares almost constantly. Frequent trading creates competition among buyers and sellers, so they must improve their prices to get trades done. But the bid-ask spread on less liquid stocks can represent a significant portion of the share price.

A well-diversified portfolio should hold somewhere around 50 to 100 stocks. This is just a ballpark figure. Sometimes it makes sense to hold more, but too many more reduces the chance stock picking will add much benefit to your portfolio. Sometimes you'll hold fewer, but too many fewer means you might not be properly diversified. Even if you're on the low end of this range and you're using an online discount broker charging a paltry $10 per trade, you're still looking at $500 in transaction costs to get your portfolio up and running. $500 is a mere 0.05 percent of a $1 million portfolio, but it's a relatively gargantuan 5 percent of a $10,000 portfolio.

Other factors might come into play when deciding whether to own individual stocks, but in this arena, size really does matter.

Another Look at Passive and Active Investing

Chapter 6 highlighted the difference between *passive* and *active* investing. To review, *active* investors strive to outperform their chosen benchmarks whereas *passive* investors aim to match their benchmarks as closely as possible.

Some of the vehicles used by global investors are actively or passively managed as well. Managers of actively managed mutual funds also attempt to outperform their benchmarks. Managers of passive funds try to follow their benchmarks closely. Actively managed funds almost always cost more because investors are paying the fund managers to make investment decisions. Passive funds tend to be cheaper because investors aren't paying for the manager's investing prowess. (Incidentally, most actively managed funds underperform their benchmarks, so "prowess" is used loosely.)

The path you take—active or passive—will significantly influence the tools you use. If you decide on the passive path, there's no need to bother with individual stocks. It would be futile for an individual investor to try and create a portfolio of stocks mimicking the performance of global equity markets. Let someone or something (i.e. mutual or exchange traded funds) else do it for you.

However, surprisingly few individual funds offer passive exposure to the entirety of global equity markets. There are myriad options providing exposure to individual pieces of global markets, but not too many covering the entire globe. Fortunately, it's fairly easy to cobble together a few pieces to create a portfolio matching the performance of global equities pretty darn closely.

If you choose the active approach, all investment options are on the table. You can choose actively managed mutual funds, passively managed mutual funds, exchange traded funds, depository receipts, ordinary shares, or any combination of these. Your top-down decisions will drive the vehicles you use.

And you needn't be wholly passive or entirely active. You can pick and choose where active decision making will add the most value to your portfolio.

MUTUAL FUNDS

They say a carpenter is only as good as his tools. The same holds true for global investors. The rest of the chapter examines the most useful investing tools.

Over $26 trillion is invested in mutual funds worldwide.[1] That's almost half the size of global equity markets! But that doesn't mean half the world's stocks are owned in mutual funds. Equity mutual funds are most common, comprising about half the mutual fund market. But there are other types of mutual funds as well. Figure 7.1 shows how the mutual fund industry breaks down by fund type in the US.

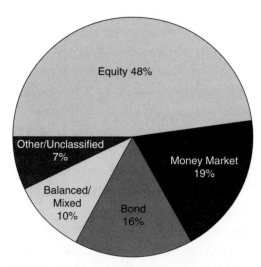

Figure 7.1   Makeup of the US Mutual Fund Market
Source: Investment Company Institute.

No single product has opened the investing world to so many people as mutual funds. If you're like most investors, you've probably owned a mutual fund or two at some point.

Sometimes you don't have a choice. Many employers restrict trading to mutual funds in retirement accounts such as 401(k)s or 403(b)s. Since these are the main investment vehicles for many folks, they're forced to invest in mutual funds. But mutual funds aren't just for retirement accounts. Mutual funds are fine options for many people in lots of different portfolios.

Often, folks aren't even aware they own mutual funds. Most of what people think of as cash in their brokerage accounts is actually invested in *money market funds.*

Definition

Money Market Fund

Many people don't realize the cash sitting in their brokerage account isn't plain old cash, earning no interest. Usually, it's earning some rate of return in a *money market fund.*

Money market funds are mutual funds investing in short-term debt instruments. Many are confined to investing in the most credit-worthy borrowers, such as US Treasury bonds or corporate bonds or commercial paper issued by highly rated companies. Occasionally, they'll have a little more leeway to try and improve returns by taking on more risk. And they're generally extremely liquid, giving investors easy access to their cash.

Most money market funds maintain a price of $1 per share. The return comes in the form of interest payments. If something goes awry in a money market fund and the share price falls below $1 per share, the fund is said to "break the buck." Needless to say, breaking the buck isn't a good thing since most investors consider cash in these accounts as extremely safe.

There are two main types of mutual funds: *open-end funds* and *closed-end funds* (exchange-traded funds are covered separately later). Shares of open-end funds are issued and redeemed continually. If you put $1,000 into an open-end fund, the fund managers invest your money and issue you shares representing $1,000 worth of the fund.

More people buying or selling shares in the fund doesn't necessarily affect the value of your shares since the manager can simply redeem shares from sellers or create shares for buyers. In the context of supply and demand, demand doesn't matter since supply is adjusted continually. As a result, shares in open-end funds always reflect the *net asset value* (or NAV) of their investments. The NAV is the total value of the fund's investments divided by the number of shares in the fund.

Closed-end funds can't issue and redeem shares so freely. They have a set number of shares outstanding, so the value of those shares doesn't necessarily reflect the value of the fund's holdings. Closed-end funds usually trade at some discount or premium to NAV. If the fund's manager is doing great and investors don't mind paying up a little to have him mange their money, shares might trade at a premium. Or if a fund's area of focus is falling out of favor and causing investors to exit a fund, shares might trade at a discount. When it comes to stocks, open-end funds are much more common, so we'll focus on those.

A mutual fund is known as a *commingled investment.*

Definition

Commingled Investments

Generally, investments can either be managed separately or they can be *commingled.* When investments are commingled, investors' funds are pooled together and managed as one large portfolio. Commingled investments hold several advantages. For smaller portfolios, commingling enables easy diversification. It lowers transaction costs. And it enables smaller portfolios to hire professional managers who might not otherwise be interested in managing their money.

But commingling isn't only for small portfolios. Many wealthy investors also commingle their funds. Hedge funds, private equity funds, and venture capital funds are commingled vehicles attracting many ultra-wealthy investors.

When you invest in a mutual fund, you're contributing to a big pool of investment dollars. In return, you get shares of the mutual fund. The value of the fund's shares is determined by the performance of the fund's holdings, less fees. Shares of a mutual fund invested in stocks will rise in value if the fund's stocks rise, and fall if the value of the fund's stocks falls. When the manager of a mutual fund trades shares, the fees associated with those trades are spread out among all the investors in the funds, lessening their impact.

Mutual Funds in a Global Portfolio

There are thousands of equity mutual funds available in the US. An increasing number of these have a global focus. On average, the amount of assets invested in equity mutual funds has grown by over 20 percent per year since 1990. But the growth of global and foreign equity mutual funds has been even more astounding: The combined assets in those funds have grown by 27 percent per year over the same period.[2]

Figure 7.2 shows the growth of mutual fund assets since 1990. The dark line shows the growth of overall mutual fund assets. But the rise of the assets in global and foreign funds (gray line) is even more impressive.

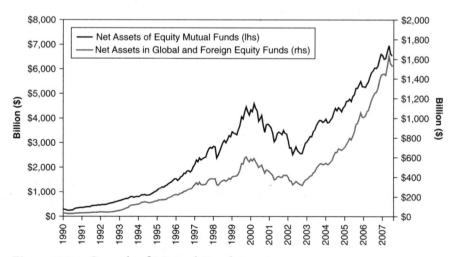

Figure 7.2   Growth of Mutual Fund Assets
Source: Thomson Datastream.

Not only have the assets invested in global and foreign mutual funds been growing by leaps and bounds, but the number of funds has skyrocketed as well. There are now over 4,800 equity mutual funds available to US investors![3] An increasing number of these invest in stocks outside the US. Figure 7.3 shows the number of global and foreign funds available in the US.

Mutual Fund Pros

Mutual funds can be a one-stop shop for global investors. Those opting for the most hands-off approach possible can simply sink their money in a global mutual fund and let the manager take it from there. There are drawbacks to mutual fund investing, but first let's cover the benefits.

Diversification for Smaller Accounts. Mutual funds are often great options for investors without huge portfolios. As mentioned earlier, transaction costs can be a significant hurdle for smaller investors. By pooling funds with others, transaction costs can be reduced for everyone involved.

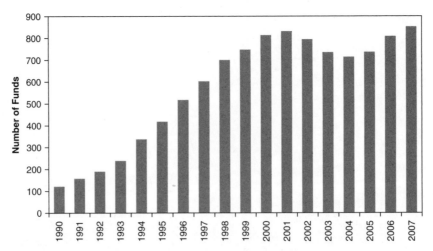

Figure 7.3   Number of Foreign and Global Mutual Funds
Source: Thomson Datastream.

But as you'll read shortly, some mutual funds tack on significant fees themselves, negating some of this benefit. Still, there are a lot of low-cost mutual funds available. Mutual funds can allow smaller investors to achieve the diversification of a larger portfolio without the associated individual transaction costs.

Access to Professional Management.   Smaller investors have trouble attracting and hiring good professional money managers. The fees they can pay for their relatively smaller pools of assets just aren't high enough to attract top talent. And given the constraints imposed by account size, professional managers couldn't add much value managing small portfolios on an individual basis anyway.

When a lot of investors put their money together, the carrot luring professional managers becomes much larger. There are few who would agree to manage 10,000 individual $10,000 accounts. The costs associated with operations, trading, servicing clients, and other account management would eat up all the fees. But put all those funds together and $100 million becomes a much more enticing number.

One-Stop Shop.   As alluded to previously, mutual funds can be a one-stop shop for global investors. A fledgling global investor can buy global fund shares and let the fund manager take it from there. Of course, you have to be willing to let the fund manager call all the shots, including the top-down country, sector, and style decisions. Some managers even take the asset allocation decision into their own hands if they can, shifting investments among stocks, bonds, and cash.

Mutual Fund Cons

Mutual funds are indeed fine tools for certain circumstances, but, as with any tool, it's not always appropriate in every situation. You wouldn't use a hammer to sand your new wood floor, nor would you always use mutual funds to get global diversification.

No Customization.   Using a mutual fund as a one-stop shop for global investing means investing in the exact same strategy as every other fund shareholder. It's impossible for a manager to customize a mutual fund for individual investors since all investor assets are pooled. If your individual situation warrants a different strategy than those of other shareholders, a mutual fund isn't going to meet your needs.

Most Are Bottom-Up.   Most mutual funds are run by bottom-up managers. As mentioned in Chapter 5, such is the way of the industry. Again, there's nothing wrong with a bottom-up approach per se, but a manager focusing on bottom-up in a global portfolio can end up with some unintended country and sector weights.

As an example, here's a look at the country and sector makeup of one well-known, bottom-up mutual fund, the Templeton Growth Fund. This fund holds over $30 billion, making it one of the largest global funds.[4] It's also one of the oldest—established by John Templeton himself in 1954. The purpose here isn't to either endorse or denigrate this particular fund. It's simply to show you how bottom-up analysis influences a global mutual fund.

Table 7.1 includes the country weights of the Templeton Growth Fund (TEPLX) relative to its benchmark, the MSCI World Index (as of March 31, 2008). The countries are ranked from largest overweight to largest underweight. The fund is most overweight to the Netherlands, South Korea, and the UK. The largest underweights are the US, Japan, and Canada.

Table 7.2 shows the same fund's sector weights (using GICS) relative to the MSCI World Index. Again, these are ranked from largest overweight to largest underweight. Judging by the sector weights, you'd have to say the fund managers are very optimistic about the prospects for Consumer Discretionary stocks and much less so about the prospects for Consumer Staples stocks. Actually, they may despise Utilities even more, but the fund already doesn't own any utilities, so it can't get any more underweight.

Why does this fund have these overweights and underweights? Does the manager think the US will perform poorly and the Netherlands will be tops? Is the manager truly bearish on Consumer

Table 7.1   Templeton Growth Fund Country Weights

Country	TEPLX Weight	MSCI World Weight	Over/Underweight
Netherlands	6.3%	1.4%	4.9%
South Korea	4.5%	0.0%	4.5%
UK	14.4%	10.6%	3.8%
Italy	4.6%	1.9%	2.7%
France	7.7%	5.4%	2.3%
Germany	6.4%	4.5%	1.9%
Singapore	1.4%	0.6%	0.8%
Russia	0.6%	0.0%	0.6%
Switzerland	4.1%	3.5%	0.5%
Mexico	0.5%	0.0%	0.5%
Taiwan	0.3%	0.0%	0.3%
Finland	1.2%	0.9%	0.3%
Sweden	1.2%	1.2%	0.0%
New Zealand	0.0%	0.1%	−0.1%
Ireland	0.3%	0.3%	−0.1%
Hong Kong	1.0%	1.1%	−0.1%
Portugal	0.0%	0.2%	−0.2%
Austria	0.0%	0.3%	−0.3%
Greece	0.0%	0.3%	−0.3%
Denmark	0.0%	0.5%	−0.5%
Norway	0.0%	0.5%	−0.5%
Belgium	0.0%	0.6%	−0.6%
Spain	0.8%	2.2%	−1.4%
Australia	0.0%	3.1%	−3.1%
Canada	0.0%	4.3%	−4.3%
Japan	4.6%	9.9%	−5.2%
US	40.2%	46.7%	−6.5%

Source: Bloomberg Finance L.P.

Staples and Utilities while bullish on Consumer Discretionary and Information Technology? Maybe, maybe not, but the stock picks have created these allocations from a bottom-up standpoint, whether or not the manager intended it.

Table 7.2   Templeton Growth Fund Sector Weights

Sectors	TEPLX Weight	MSCI World Weight	Difference
Consumer Discretionary	20.0%	9.7%	10.4%
Information Technology	16.8%	10.4%	6.3%
Telecommunication Services	7.9%	4.6%	3.3%
Health Care	11.6%	8.8%	2.7%
Industrials	13.7%	11.8%	1.9%
Energy	7.9%	11.1%	−3.2%
Financials	18.0%	22.1%	−4.1%
Utilities	0.0%	4.7%	−4.7%
Materials	2.5%	7.8%	−5.3%
Consumer Staples	1.6%	9.0%	−7.3%

Source: Bloomberg Finance L.P.

Remember, this isn't a static allocation. By the time you read this, the weights shown will have undoubtedly changed. But by definition, a bottom-up portfolio is less concerned with sector and country exposure than it is with stock picking.

Transparency.   When buying an actively managed mutual fund, you're never exactly sure what you're getting. You'll know what type of fund it is, a thing or two about the manager, and the fund's historical performance. Managers are required to divulge that information. But mutual funds aren't very forthcoming when it comes to their current investments. Most mutual funds report their holdings once a quarter. So four times a year they provide snapshots of the stocks they own, as of the day they report.

But what happens in between those times is known only to the folks at the fund. This doesn't provide much transparency for investors. Fund managers are also known to "dress up" their portfolios when it comes time to report their holdings to make their investments look more attractive. So the strategy reflected in the snapshot might vary from the strategy employed at other times.

Fees.   Some mutual funds carry hefty sales charges. These are known as *load* funds. The amounts and when they're paid vary depending on the class of shares purchased. Typically, "Class A" shares are *front-end loaded*—the sales charge comes right off the top when you buy the shares. "Class B" shares are typically *back-end loaded,* meaning the charge comes when you sell the shares (a nice little treat to look forward to). There are other fee structures associated with other share classes as well. By contrast, *no-load funds* don't have sales charges. These have become increasingly popular. Not only is the prospect of avoiding fees appealing, but on balance, load funds don't perform any better than no-load funds, making the sales charge even less palatable.

However, both load and no-load funds still charge ongoing management fees. These are called *expense ratios.* They will vary quite a bit from fund to fund. The passively managed funds I mentioned earlier tend to have lower expense ratios because the manager is just trying to match the performance of the fund's benchmark, which usually isn't too difficult a task. Expense ratios on actively managed funds tend to be much higher since you're paying the fund managers to make investment decisions.

Tax Inefficient.   Another drawback: Mutual fund investors don't get the benefit of realizing losses on their stocks to offset gains at tax time. But there's another reason mutual funds are tax inefficient: Mutual fund investors can end up paying taxes on gains they never received!

Mutual funds distribute capital gains to shareholders regardless of how long they've owned their shares or how the fund has performed since the shares were purchased. Imagine a fund had a great five-year stretch resulting in significant gains in the fund's stocks. Then you decide to buy your first shares in the fund. If the fund manager then realized those earlier gains and couldn't offset them with losses within the fund, all existing shareholders (including you who just bought into the fund) would receive a capital gains distribution. If you bought shares of the fund in a taxable account, you might pay for those gains even though your specific shares hadn't gone up at all.

EXCHANGE-TRADED FUNDS (ETFs)

If you think the growth in mutual funds has been impressive, the growth in exchange-traded funds will really blow you away. ETFs are a much newer vehicle than mutual funds. The first US mutual fund was introduced way back in the 1920s, but ETFs didn't come on the scene in the US until 1993. There are now over 600 ETFs here, holding over $600 billion in assets.[5] This is a drop in the bucket compared to the amount invested in mutual funds, but if the ETF market continues growing at its current pace, ETFs will catch up before long. Since 2000, ETF investments have grown by over 37 percent per year. And the number of ETFs available has grown by 70 percent annually![6]

ETFs and mutual funds are alike in many ways, but they have some important differences. The most striking is how they trade. Mutual funds are bought and sold once at the end of the trading day, whereas ETFs trade throughout the day, just like regular stocks. ETFs share some similarities with both open- and closed-end mutual funds. Their prices aren't directly determined by the NAV of the fund's holdings, but they have a unique feature that keeps the price from straying too far from NAV.

Definition

Creation Units

ETF shares can trade at premiums or discounts to the value of the assets owned by the fund. But there's a tool in place that limits the deviation from NAV. ETF shares are redeemed or issued via *creation units*. A *creation unit* contains the shares that make up the ETF. You can't actually trade in individual ETF shares for the fund's underlying assets. But you could if you had enough dough to buy an entire creation unit.

Let's say a fund's creation-unit size is 50,000 shares. You could buy 50,000 individual shares of the ETF and trade them for the underlying assets. Or you could buy a creation unit's worth of underlying assets and have ETF shares issued. This might seem pointless since few individuals would ever think of buying or selling ETFs this way. But creation units help keep the prices of ETF shares near NAV.

How? It's because of the arbitrage opportunity. If an ETF trades at a big premium or discount to NAV, big institutions can profit. If ETF shares trade at a significant premium, a large institution could short a creation unit worth of ETFs, buy a creation unit worth of underlying stocks, convert the underlying stocks to ETF shares, and deliver those to close the short position. If ETF shares trade at a discount, big institutions could do the opposite. Most institutions (and individuals for that matter) like free money, so they're not likely to let a meaningful premium or discount last for long.

The vast majority of ETFs are passively managed, so they're intended to match their benchmarks as closely as possible. As mentioned in Chapter 6, funds don't necessarily own all the stocks in their indexes. Because different funds use different techniques to mimic indexes, two funds managed by different people can perform differently, even if they track the same index. But over the long term, these differences should be minimal if the fund managers are doing their jobs right.

Passively managed ETFs will likely dominate the industry for the foreseeable future, but they're about to get some company. ETF managers have received the thumbs-up to market actively managed ETFs. These will be run like actively managed mutual funds (likely including the higher fees), but they'll trade throughout the day like regular ETFs.

One issue likely to inhibit the growth of active ETFs is the reporting requirement. Unlike mutual funds, ETFs are required to report their holdings daily. This isn't a big deal for passively managed funds since their holdings largely mirror their benchmarks. But active managers like to play things closer to the vest. So starting an actively managed ETF isn't always an attractive option for fund managers.

ETFs in a Global Portfolio

ETFs offer a few big advantages for global investors. One of the most significant is the wide variety of funds available. There are broad ETFs covering the whole world (or large portions of it) and focused ETFs covering specific countries and sectors (even sectors within countries!). So a global investor utilizing a top-down approach can use ETFs to gain exposure to an entire country or region or make more targeted investment decisions.

Table 7.3 ETFs Exposure

Global	Broad Foreign/Region	Country	Sector
iShares MSCI ACWI	iShares MSCI EAFE	SPDR Trust Series 1 (US)	iShares S&P Global Cons Disc
iShares S&P Global 100	iShares MSCI EM	SPDR S&P China	iShares S&P Global Cons Staples
SPDR Global Titans	iShares MSCI Pacific ex-Japan	iShares MSCI Australia	iShares S&P Global Energy
Vanguard Total World Stock	SPDR MSCI ACWI ex-US	iShares MSCI Brazil	iShares S&P Global Healthcare
	SPDR S&P World ex-US	iShares MSCI Canada	iShares S&P Global Materials
	SPDR S&P EM	iShares MSCI France	iShares S&P Global Technology
	SPDR S&P Emerging Asia Pacific	iShares MSCI Germany	iShares S&P Global Telecom
	SPDR S&P Emerging Europe	iShares MSCI Hong Kong	iShares S&P Global Utilities
	SPDR S&P Emerging Latin America	iShares MSCI Japan	
	Vanguard FTSE All-World ex-US	iShares MSCI Mexico	
	Vanguard Europe Pacific	iShares MSCI Singapore	
	Vanguard EM	iShares MSCI South Korea	
	Vanguard European	iShares MSCI Sweden	
	Vanguard Pacific	iShares MSCI UK	

Source: Bloomberg Finance L.P.

Table 7.3 includes some examples of ETFs providing exposure to different regions, countries, and sectors. A comprehensive list would span several pages. But note how few truly global options are available. As of this writing, the only ETFs tracking any of the well-constructed global indexes mentioned in Chapter 6 is the iShares MSCI ACWI Index Fund. But it's fairly easy to piece together other ETFs to achieve broad global exposure. All you need to do is buy individual country ETFs in proportion to their weights in your benchmark. Not every country has an ETF, but there are enough to build a portfolio that tracks global benchmarks pretty closely. You could do the same by buying individual sector ETFs. But these would have to be global, and the options are limited.

You'll notice the aforementioned global ETF and many of the country-specific ETFs are produced by iShares. Most of the non-US iShares ETFs use MSCI indexes as their benchmarks. So if you plan on making extensive use of iShares, it's probably a good idea to choose one of the MSCI indexes as your benchmark as well. It's not imperative, but it can't hurt to use the same framework as the folks managing the funds.

ETF Oligarchy

In the US, the growing ETF market is dominated by a few large managers. The biggest ETF on the planet in terms of assets under management is the SPDR Trust, Series 1 (aka "Spider"), with over $75 billion in net assets as of this writing.

The Spider ETF tracks the performance of the S&P 500 Index. It was the first ETF listed in the US back in 1993. Spider and other ETFs in the SPDR family are managed by State Street Global Advisors. The SPDR family includes many globally focused ETFs, as well as a number of useful funds tracking individual sectors both inside and outside the US.

Spider might be the biggest individual ETF, but if you add all the ETF assets from all families, iShares take the cake. The iShares family has over a quarter-trillion dollars invested in its equity ETFs alone. In keeping with the global theme, iShares are managed by Barclays Global Investors, a US-subsidiary of UK-based Barclays Bank.

Vanguard is also a major ETF player. Most of Vanguard's ETFs track US stocks of one kind or another. But Vanguard does have a few non-US options.

PowerShares made a name for itself in the ETF business in 1999 with the introduction of the PowerShares QQQ ETF (known as the triple Qs until the fund's ticker symbol was changed from three Qs to four Qs). The now quadruple Qs track the NASDAQ 100 index, which includes the 100 largest companies in the tech-laden NASDAQ index.

ETF Pros

As with mutual funds, these tools do have their strong points, as well as their drawbacks. First, the benefits.

Variety. The variety of ETFs enables investors to make fairly precise investment decisions while maintaining diversification. This is especially useful in some of the smaller countries and sectors.

If you're excited about the Spanish market, you might want to overweight Spanish stocks in your portfolio. But Spain makes up a small portion of global benchmarks, so a significant overweight might mean putting just a few percent of your portfolio in Spain. You could buy one or two Spanish stocks, but you'd run the risk of stock-specific issues trumping your country decision, even if Spanish stocks go through the roof. Instead, you could buy an ETF tracking the broad Spanish market and do away with stock-specific risk.

Low Cost. Because most are passively managed, ETFs tend to have lower management fees—much lower than most actively managed mutual funds. For instance, the expense ratio for the Spider ETF is a tiny 0.095 percent, while the expense ratios on an actively managed mutual fund investing in US stocks can be as high as a few percent.

Transparency. Unlike mutual funds, ETFs are required to report their holdings daily. As a result, ETFs are more transparent. Greater transparency makes it easier to monitor what's going on in your portfolio.

Tax Efficient. ETFs are fairly tax efficient. Similar to individual stocks, ETFs allow investors to offset capital gains with capital losses. If your Canadian ETF lets you down, you can sell that particular ETF to offset gains you might have realized elsewhere. But be careful about deviating too much from your benchmark. Unless you find another investment that gives you exposure to Canadian stocks, your country weights might be off kilter.

ETFs offer another tax advantage over mutual funds. Since mutual funds issue and redeem shares continually, an exodus by investors from a particular fund forces the fund manager to sell some of its holdings to raise cash for redemptions. This can mean realizing capital gains, which are then spread among investors. ETFs don't issue and redeem their shares the way mutual funds do. So an exodus from ETF shares doesn't necessitate any selling by the fund manager. As a result, unsuspecting shareholders aren't left with the tax bill.

ETF Cons

Those are some of the selling points. But there are instances when ETFs fall short as investing tools.

Still Not as Tax Efficient as Individual Stocks. ETFs can be more tax efficient than mutual funds, but they're still not as tax efficient as owning individual stocks. At any given time, an ETF will include some stocks with gains and some stocks with losses. Since the downtrodden shares are held within the ETF, shareholders can't specifically use the losses to their advantage.

Transaction Costs. This is where some mutual funds have the upper hand on ETFs. Because ETFs trade like individual stocks, they have the same transaction costs. Brokers charge commissions to buy and sell them. They have a bid-ask spread like individual stocks as well. In contrast, no-load mutual funds don't carry either of these costs if you buy them directly from the fund company.

Despite the transaction costs, owning ETFs in a smaller portfolio can still be a good idea even if owning individual stocks isn't. Why? Because most ETFs are already well diversified, so you don't have to buy dozens of them to diversify your portfolio like you do with individual stocks. Fewer ETFs to purchase means you pay less in transaction costs.

DEPOSITORY RECEIPTS

The next two investment vehicles covered, *depository receipts* and *ordinary shares*, involve purchasing shares in individual firms. This may or may not be your best option, depending on the factors outlined earlier in this chapter. If you're leaning toward using mutual funds or ETFs in your global portfolio, it's still not a bad idea to know something about buying individual foreign shares. If it's not already, someday your portfolio might be substantial enough to go this route.

American Depository Receipts (better known as ADRs) are an easy way for US investors to buy shares of individual foreign firms. ADRs trade on US exchanges, so most are just as easy to buy and sell as US stocks. The name of the firm you're investing in might divulge its foreign origins (there's no mystery to the domicile of companies like France Telecom or Korea Electric Power), but otherwise, you might not notice the difference between ADRs and shares of a US firm.

There are different types of ADRs, as you'll read, but many have ticker symbols just like US stocks, are registered with the US Securities and Exchange Commission (SEC), pay ADR holders dividends in US dollars, and use US accounting and reporting standards.

The ADR market isn't some small obscure niche. As of this writing, there was over $2 trillion invested in ADRs here. They're not new, either. ADRs date back to 1927 when UK retailer Selfridges listed the first one. And as investors have increasingly embraced global investment opportunities, interest in ADRs has soared.

US regulations for publicly traded firms are more onerous than in many other countries, especially since the passing of the Public Company Accounting Reform and Investor Protection Act of 2002 (better known as Sarbanes-Oxley). The relatively harsh environment for companies listed in the US has led some foreign firms to terminate their ADR programs, but overall, capital raised through ADRs has been going through the roof. In 2007, foreign firms raised over $57 billion by issuing ADRs, up from less than $8 billion in 2002. Figure 7.4 shows the growth in cash raised by foreign companies listing ADRs on US exchanges.

The big upswing is largely due to firms in emerging markets tapping US capital. Many of the most actively traded ADRs emanate from emerging markets including Petrobras (Brazil), Baidu.com (China), OAO Gazprom (Russia), and América Móvil (Mexico).

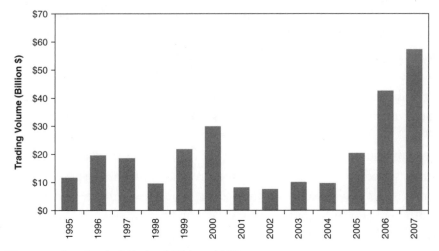

Figure 7.4   Capital Raised Using ADRs
Source: ADR.com.

ADRs represent ownership in foreign companies. Each ADR is backed by a set number of ordinary shares trading in a firm's home market. The number of shares represented by each ADR is known as the *depository receipt ratio*. Depository banks such as JP Morgan, Bank of New York, Citigroup, and Deutsche Bank collect the ordinary shares backing ADRs and issue ADRs in the US market. Owing a single ADR in Chinese oil company PetroChina is like owning 100 ordinary shares in China. So the depository receipt ratio is 1:100.

ADRs are quoted, bought, and sold in US dollars, so there's no need to worry about converting currency. But currencies still impact ADRs. ADRs are subject to the same supply and demand forces as any other stock, but there are more moving pieces with an ADR. Since ADRs represent a number of ordinary shares, the price of an ADR is strongly influenced by price changes in the ordinary shares and changes in exchange rates.

An example: Let's say you bought 100 shares of UK telecom company Vodafone Group PLC. The depository receipt ratio for Vodafone is 1:10, so owning one ADR represents 10 shares in the UK. If Vodafone shares are trading at £1.50 in London and the exchange rate between the US dollar and the pound sterling is $2.00 per pound, Vodafone ADRs should trade around $30 per ADR. If Vodafone's local shares rise in value or the pound rises against the dollar, the price of the ADRs should rise as well.

They don't always move in perfect unison. The time difference alone means US investors will be trading ADRs while UK markets are closed, so there will be some disparity between the price of the ADRs and the value of the shares they represent. But similar to creation units with ETFs, large institutions can have ordinary shares turned into ADRs or vice versa, so the arbitrage opportunity keeps the prices from getting too far out of whack.

Firms list ADRs for several reasons. Some raise new capital by issuing ADRs. Others don't raise new money but are looking to increase their exposure in the all-important US market. ADRs also allow firms to attract new shareholders who might not otherwise venture abroad to buy their shares. And some companies might issue ADRs to make it easier to acquire US companies.

On the Level

There are four levels of ADRs:

- **Level I:** The most basic. Level I ADRs aren't listed on US exchanges. Instead, they trade in the *over-the-counter* market. As a result, most have funny-looking ticker symbols with five letters ending in "Y." Companies with only Level I ADRs aren't required to file quarterly or annual reports or use US accounting standards. Because Level I ADRs are the easiest and least costly, they're also the most abundant. Of the 1,429 ADRs, 974 of them are Level I ADRs.[7]
- **Level II:** Companies listing Level II ADRs file a registration statement with the SEC. These companies must file annual reports and use US accounting standards. Level II ADRs are also listed on exchanges, which may make them more attractive to investors.

- **Level III:** Level III ADRs require the most work for foreign firms. Issuing Level I or Level II ADRs means taking some shares from the local market, putting them with a depository bank, and having ADRs issued. In contrast, companies issuing Level III ADRs actually raise cash through the offering by issuing entirely new shares to put on deposit. So selling Level III ADRs requires many of the same regulatory steps as a new share offering by a US firm.
- **144A:** 144A ADRs are available only to Qualified Institutional Buyers (QIBs). Since this is a market for professional investors only, the reporting requirements are much more lax.

Other DRs

Depository receipts aren't exclusive to America. Depository receipts are traded in many countries. Outside the US, the most common variants are Global Depository Receipts (aka GDRs), which trade on exchanges in London, Luxembourg, Frankfurt, Dubai, and Singapore, among others.

ADR Pros

So what are the reasons to trade ADRs?

They Trade Like US Stocks.   ADRs are usually the easiest way to buy shares of foreign companies. From a US investor's perspective, owning ADRs is scarcely different than owning US stocks.

US Reporting and Accounting.   Companies with Level II and Level III ADRs are registered with the US Securities and Exchange Commission and are required to use either US or approved international accounting standards. Level II ADR issuers file annual reports. Level III issuers file both quarterly and annual reports. Reporting and accounting for Level I issuers are less stringent. But international accounting standards are frequently robust, so a Level I listing doesn't mean you should necessarily shy away from a firm.

Cost. If you're looking to buy shares in a foreign company, and you have the option of buying either ADRs or ordinary shares on the firm's local exchange, there's a good chance buying the ADR is the cheaper option. Buying ordinary shares is easy these days, but often the transaction costs are higher than trading in the US. Since ADRs are listed on US exchanges, you can take advantage of the low transaction costs here.

The one exception here has to do with trading volume. Some ADRs don't trade much even if the ordinary shares do. As mentioned earlier in this chapter, it can be more expensive to buy illiquid shares, so at times you might do better with the ordinary shares.

No Need to Convert Currency. As you'll read later, buying ordinary shares on foreign exchanges requires converting your dollars to another currency. Converting currencies usually involves a fee (of course), which adds to the cost of the purchase or sale. Since ADRs trade in US dollars, you get to skip this sometimes costly step.

No Custody Issues. Custody concerns are less prevalent these days than they have been in the past, but ADRs negate the issue entirely because shares are held at large, reputable US institutions.

ADR Cons

And now for the cons.

Limited Options. Even though the ADR market is big and the options many, there are far more global stocks than there are ADRs. Even some of the largest foreign firms don't have ADRs, so the only way to invest in them directly is through ordinary shares.

For example, Japanese firms have made the most use of ADRs. In total, 170 Japanese companies have ADRs trading in the US, more than any other country.[8] But that's less than 10 percent of the number of companies listed on the first section of the Tokyo Stock Exchange. Additionally, companies listing ADRs are usually relatively large since bigger companies are more likely to draw the interest of

US investors. So limiting yourself to ADRs often means adopting a large-cap bias as well.

ORDINARY SHARES

Last, there's ordinary individual stocks—but with a twist. You are probably familiar with the ease of buying US stocks. Just pick up the phone and call your broker. Or log on to your broker's website and place a trade. Guess what—you can do the same with many foreign stocks. It's true. Buying shares on foreign exchanges is almost as easy as buying US shares. Just about any full-service brokerage firm can access ordinary shares in foreign markets. Even discount brokers are getting into the global game. Clients of discount broker Charles Schwab & Co. have access to stocks in 45 foreign countries. And E*Trade Securities now offers online trading in six foreign markets and five currencies.

But even though buying foreign ordinary shares is easy, it can also be costly. Buying ordinary shares can involve several layers of fees. There's usually a commission charged by the US broker. There's often a fee to convert US dollars into whatever currency is needed to purchase shares. Often US brokers place the trade through foreign correspondent brokers. Naturally, they charge a fee, too. And some foreign countries charge taxes or other fees to complete the transaction. All these fees mean portfolio size is an even more important consideration in a global portfolio.

Ordinary Shares Pros

So why buy ordinary shares in foreign markets if there are so many options here in the US of A?

Tons of Options. As mentioned in Chapter 6, there are over 25,000 investable companies in the world. About 17,000 or so are outside the US. Not all of these are available to US investors, thanks to regulations, foreign ownership limits, and capital controls in some countries. But there are still plenty to choose from.

Ordinary Shares Cons

That's the upside. But buying ordinary shares does come with drawbacks that can be pricey or just confusing.

Costs.   Again, buying foreign ordinary shares can be expensive. If you're placing small trades, the cost of buying stocks in some countries can exceed 10 percent of your investment. This makes buying foreign ordinary shares prohibitive in smaller accounts.

Reporting and Accounting Standards.   Reporting and accounting standards in many developed countries are on par with those in the US. But standards in some emerging countries aren't as good. Make sure you can get accurate and timely information about the company you're investing in.

Language.   Even great information isn't useful if you can't understand it. Many foreign companies issue press releases, earnings announcements, and other information in English even if they don't list shares here in the US. But not all do. Getting information you can understand is a challenge with some foreign stocks.

The Global View

The investing tools you'll use to build your global portfolio are fairly simple. Using them effectively is the real challenge. Your decision about which is most appropriate can make the difference between sailing the global seas and being stuck in the doldrums.

You might decide to build a global portfolio using just one of these tools, or you might find that a combination of them is right for you. As mentioned, the size of your portfolio and the time you want to dedicate to global investing will help determine the most appropriate investment vehicles. No matter which you use in your portfolio, don't forget the earlier lessons about risk control and diversification.

The Currency
Effect

Maybe you don't love money. But judging by the fact you're reading this book, you probably have some affinity for the stuff. (Good for you!) And if you're looking to invest, you probably have some lying around. You might not be the type who craves mega wealth. But even if you don't aspire to become the next JD Rockefeller or JP Morgan (or JR Ewing of *Dallas* fame for that matter), I'd wager you care more than a smidge about money—or at least currency.

Face it: We'd be in a heap of trouble without currency. It's the most important financial innovation in the last four thousand years—period. Without it, the vast majority of financial transactions would be virtually impossible, and we'd probably have to revert to the barter system. Admittedly, it would be amusing to watch grocery clerks try to make change for a chicken. And we'd all love to pay our taxes by sending the IRS boxes of dried herring. But a few hilarious episodes aside, we're much better off with a common medium of exchange.

THE ALMIGHTY DOLLAR, EURO, POUND, RINGGIT, BAHT . . .

Forget chickens and beads. Today, we've gotten so advanced we barely use physical currency. Dollar bills and coins have been replaced by electronic bits whizzing between bank accounts. Still, we have over $792 billion of physical US currency in circulation,[1] most of which is floating around somewhere outside the US. The US dollar is so widely used and has been so stable over the years it's become the global currency of choice. So much so, when people refer to the "dollar," they're almost always referring to the US dollar, even though there are many different varieties.

Internationally traded commodities like oil and gold are priced in dollars. And people in many countries regularly accept dollars as payment for goods and services. In fact, some countries have gone so far as to jettison their currencies entirely and rely solely on the greenback. But most countries have their own currencies, so knowing a thing or two about exchange rates is important for global investors.

Exchange Rates.   The value of one currency relative to another is the *exchange rate*. One US dollar in 2008 bought about one-half a pound sterling, two-thirds of a euro, or one hundred yen. Pick any two currencies, and there's an exchange rate between them.

Forty years ago, this chapter would have been pointless. Back then, currencies were important, but exchange rates weren't. The US

Name that Currency

There are almost as many currencies as there are countries. Many currencies have unique names, such as the Vietnamese dong or the Polish zloty. But a surprising number share the same name. The US isn't alone in calling its currency the "dollar." Australia, New Zealand, Singapore, and Canada are just a few nations that refer to their currencies as dollars. In total, there are 22 different dollar types used by 58 different countries and territories. The franc has also been a popular name, as has the dinar, the peso, and the pound. Table 8.1 shows the many currencies with these popular names.

Table 8.1   Common Currency Names

Dollar	Franc	Dinar	Peso	Pound
Australian	Belgian	Algerian	Argentinean	Cypriot
Bahamian	Burundian	Bahraini	Bolivian	Egyptian
Barbadian	Central African	Croatian	Chilean	Falkland
Belize	Comorian	Iraqi	Colombian	Gibraltar
Bermudian	Djiboutian	Jordanian	Cuban	Lebanese
Brunei	French	Kuwaiti	Dominican Republic	Maltese
Canadian	Guinean	Libyan	Guinea-Bissau	Pound Sterling (UK)
Cayman Islands	Luxembourgian	Macedonian	Mexican	St Helena
East Caribbean	Malagasy	Serbian	Philippine	Sudanese
Fijian	Malian	Tunisian	Uruguayan	Syrian
Guyanese	Pacific			
Hong Kong	Rwandan			
Jamaican	Swiss			
Liberian				
Namibian				
New Taiwan				
New Zealand				
Singaporean				
Solomon Island				
Trinidad and				
Tobago				
US				
Zimbabwean				

was on the gold standard, and most foreign currencies were fixed to the dollar, so exchange rates rarely changed. But once the US left the gold standard and the dollar became *fiat currency*, global currency values began fluctuating. The dollar has remained the undisputed King of Currencies, but now its value changes by the second.

Definition

Fiat Currency

Why does currency have value? As explained in this chapter, currencies have at times been tied to commodities such as gold, so their value was derived from the fact currencies could be traded for a predetermined amount of something else. But today, most currencies have value simply because governments say they do. These are known as *fiat currencies*. The US government says US dollars are legal tender, so the market treats them as such. Some fiat currencies don't even have the official backing of the government, so it's the market itself and faith in the issuing institutions that give these currencies value. For example, several of Scotland's largest banks issue pound notes, which aren't considered legal tender but are accepted as currency throughout the UK.

Like anything else traded in free markets, exchange rates are determined by supply and demand. Technically, central banks have monopolies on controlling the supply of currencies, but there are many factors affecting demand. Things like economic growth rates, inflation, capital flows, and a host of other factors impact a currency's value. And, as covered further in this chapter, governments play big roles as well. But for freely traded currencies, one of the most important factors driving exchange rates is differences in interest rates between countries.

The relationship between interest rate expectations and exchange rates is illustrated in Figure 8.1. This chart shows the difference in investors' expectations for short-term interest rates (as measured using derivatives known as *overnight index swaps*) in the US and Japan, along with the exchange rate between the US dollar and the yen. When investors expect the difference between US and Japanese rates to widen, the dollar generally gains versus the yen. When investors expect the difference in interest rates to narrow, the dollar loses ground.

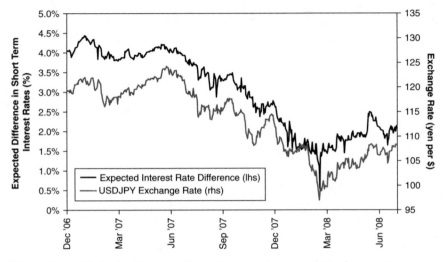

Figure 8.1   Relative Interest Rate Expectations and Exchange Rates
Source: Bloomberg Finance L.P.

This works because dollar-denominated assets, especially debt securities such as short-term government bonds, become relatively more attractive when US interest rates are high compared to Japanese rates and relatively less attractive when interest rates are expected to be lower compared to Japan. This relationship isn't exclusive to the US and Japan. Expected interest rate differentials are significant drivers of exchange rates among most major currencies.

Thar Was Gold in Them Thar Currencies

From 1944 to 1971, the US was on the gold standard. Every dollar was worth a set amount of yellow metal—$35 would buy exactly one ounce. Since gold is in limited supply and many people value it, linking the dollar to gold made it more stable—an important trait as the world economy emerged from World War II.

(Continued)

Allied countries hoped a more stable international currency system would facilitate global trade. Under the Bretton Woods system—named for Bretton Woods, New Hampshire, where the United Nations Monetary and Financial Conference took place—allied countries agreed to fix their exchange rates with the US dollar, effectively making the US dollar the currency for the entire world!

With the gold standard in place, it should have been impossible to increase money supply without changing the amount of gold each dollar was worth or finding more gold (which actually happened during the gold rush of the mid-1800s, another period when the dollar was linked to gold). But the US began printing more dollars than it had gold to back. Eventually, the system broke down when foreign governments began demanding gold for their dollars. On August 15, 1971, Richard Nixon ceased the dollar's convertibility to gold, ending the gold standard.

CURRENCY TRIVIA

Currency markets are quite different from stock markets. Size is one distinguishing feature. The aggregate value of global stocks is large, but currency markets are huge. Every day, more currency and currency instruments trade hands than all the world's stocks and bonds combined. In total, $3.2 trillion of currency-related transactions take place daily.[2]

Currency markets are also different because currency trades are always done in pairs. If you buy one currency, you sell another. The dollar is by far the most frequently traded currency and usually accounts for one half the pair. If you want to convert Mexican pesos to Swedish krona, you're probably better off converting your pesos to dollars first and your dollars to krona because the dollar market is most liquid.

The most-traded currency pair is the US dollar/euro, accounting for 27 percent of daily trades.[3] This isn't too surprising considering the US and Eurozone countries account for almost half the global economy.[4] Table 8.2 shows the daily currency market turnover by currency pair.

There are pretty much always some stock markets open, but none of the major stock markets stay open around the clock. So at

Table 8.2   Currency Pairs

Currency Pair	Daily Turnover (billion $)	% Share
US dollar/euro	$840	27.3%
US dollar/yen	$397	12.9%
US dollar/sterling	$361	11.7%
US dollar/Australian dollar	$175	5.7%
US dollar/Swiss franc	$143	4.6%
US dollar/Canadian dollar	$115	3.7%
US dollar/Swedish krona	$ 56	1.8%
US dollar/other	$572	18.6%
Euro/yen	$ 70	2.3%
Euro/sterling	$ 64	2.1%
Euro/Swiss franc	$ 54	1.8%
Euro/other	$112	3.6%
Other currency pairs	$122	4.0%

Source: Bank for International Settlements.

certain times of the day, there are stocks you can't buy or sell easily on exchanges. By contrast, currencies trade 24 hours a day in countries all over the world. As the Earth turns on its axis, currency traders chase the sun west. They start their day in Australia and quickly move to Singapore, Japan, and Hong Kong. Then on to Europe, where most of the world's currency trades take place. Over a third of global currency trades are executed in the UK.[5] Finally, traders finish in the US, only to have trading move seamlessly to Australia once again. You can see the most common locales for currency trading in Table 8.3.

What's With All This Currency Trading?

Currency trading is abundant because currencies facilitate everything from trade to travel to investing. If you buy a bushel of bananas from Guatemala, at some point your dollars are probably converted to quetzals to pay the local growers. Similarly, if you buy a Turkish stock directly on the Istanbul Stock Exchange, you need some lira. But many investors treat currencies as an asset class of their own, buying

Table 8.3 Geographic Distribution of Currency Trading

Country	Amount (billion $)	% Share
UK	$1,359	34.1%
US	$ 664	16.6%
Switzerland	$ 242	6.1%
Japan	$ 238	6.0%
Singapore	$ 231	5.8%
Hong Kong	$ 175	4.4%
Australia	$ 170	4.3%
France	$ 120	3.0%
Germany	$ 99	2.5%
Denmark	$ 86	2.2%
Canada	$ 60	1.5%
Russia	$ 50	1.3%
Belgium	$ 48	1.2%
Luxembourg	$ 43	1.1%
Sweden	$ 42	1.1%
Other	$ 363	9.1%

Source: Bank for International Settlements.

and selling to profit from exchange rate changes. Considering the size of currency markets and all the different factors affecting currency values, figuring which direction currencies are going to move is a difficult task. But that doesn't keep people from trying.

Some of the brightest minds in finance regularly try forecasting currency movements with very mixed results. Investor George Soros famously "broke" the Bank of England by betting against pound sterling, making himself over a billion dollars in the process. But most investors aren't as successful. Fortunately, even though currencies are extremely important, forecasting currency movements is in no way a prerequisite for global investing. In fact, as you'll read in this chapter, you might discover you'll be better off ignoring currencies entirely.

Soros: 1, Bank of England: 0

Before the advent of the euro as a common European currency, there was the European Exchange Rate Mechanism (ERM). The ERM was established to stabilize exchange rates among the many different European currencies. Under the ERM, currencies could fluctuate, but only within a narrow range. If currencies moved too much, the central banks of those countries were obligated to take steps to bring their currencies back into compliance. The UK was late to join the ERM but eventually did so with reluctance in 1990.

By 1992, cracks were developing in the system. Even though exchange rates were effectively fixed, central banks could set their own interest rates. Rates were on the rise in Germany as Germany's Bundesbank sought to combat the uncertainty and inflationary pressures caused by the reunification of East and West Germany. But the Bank of England didn't follow suit with rate hikes of its own, and the pound came under significant pressure. Currency speculators, including Soros, took notice and placed huge bets that the Bank of England would not be able to keep the pound within the range required by the ERM and the currency would eventually be devalued. In all, Soros bet over $10 billion the pound would fall.

On September 16, 1992, a date now known as "Black Wednesday," Soros got his wish. In a series of desperate moves to support the pound, the Bank of England raised interest rates dramatically and poured significant reserves into currency markets. But by the end of the day, Soros and his cohorts prevailed as the pound fell sharply versus the Deutsche Mark, and the Bank of England announced the UK would leave the ERM.

WRANGLING EXCHANGE RATES

Earlier, I mentioned exchange rates are set in free markets by supply and demand. This isn't entirely true. Although the part about supply and demand is accurate, classifying currency markets as "free" is somewhat of a stretch. Governments (I'll lump governments and central banks together here) can have enormous influence over currency markets, and many actively buy and sell currencies to try to keep exchange rates where they want. Even governments with the most hands-off approach have been known to try nudging currencies one direction or another.

Generally, currencies are either pegged, managed, or allowed to float. But the lines separating these categories are quite blurry. And governments often change their approaches to currency management, so a currency that was once pegged might be allowed to float or vice versa. Knowing how these approaches differ is important to knowing not only how your investments are performing, but they also might influence where you decide to invest.

Pegged Currencies

Pegged currencies are the most strictly managed.

> ### Definition
>
> **Pegged Exchange Rate**
>
> When one currency is *pegged* to another, the exchange rate between the two barely changes. For instance, the Hong Kong dollar/US dollar exchange rate has been pegged at HK$7.80 since 1983. Similarly, the Nepalese rupee/Indian rupee exchange rate is pegged at NPR1.60.

Most countries that peg do so with the US dollar, but not always. Some are pegged to other currencies or even baskets of currencies. Governments keep their currencies pegged by buying and selling them in currency markets. If market forces cause the exchange rate of a pegged currency to fall, the government buys its currency and sells the other to bring the exchange rate back to the pegged value. If the exchange rate rises, the government does the opposite.

It takes a lot of capital to do all this buying and selling, so countries heavily involved in currency markets usually have substantial reserves of foreign currencies, which they use to intervene in currency markets. China has been pegging its currency for years and has built up foreign currency reserves of over $1.8 trillion—more than any other country. Even though the yen isn't a pegged currency, Japan built up substantial reserves when it was more active in currency markets. Today, Japan has foreign currency reserves of almost $1 trillion.

China's De-Pegging

Up until 2005, the Chinese yuan was pegged to the US dollar. But as China's economy grew, the international community began to view China's US dollar peg as an unfair advantage in global trade. China was admitted into the World Trade Organization in 2001, so foreign governments and trade groups expect China to play by established rules, including those prohibiting currency manipulation. Most believed the dollar peg kept the yuan artificially undervalued, and, thus, made Chinese goods unfairly cheap. So in 2005, China abandoned its dollar peg and pegged the yuan to a basket of currencies that includes not only dollars but euros, yen, and presumably a number of other currencies (the Chinese government doesn't disclose the actual composition of the basket). Many still believe the yuan is undervalued, but its gradual appreciation since the policy change has appeased many critics.

There are many reasons a country might peg its currency. A primary reason is stability. Frequently, countries that peg have small or unstable economies. Pegging their currencies to those of larger economies can make their currencies more stable. This is especially important when it comes to attracting foreign investment because a wildly fluctuating currency means the value of assets owned by foreigners will fluctuate wildly as well. A country might also peg if most of its trade takes place in a single currency. For instance, many Middle Eastern countries peg their currencies to the dollar not only for stability but also because their main export is oil, which is priced in dollars.

Problematic Pegs.   However, currency pegs can be problematic. Pegging to another country's currency also means following that country's monetary policy or putting strict capital controls in place. Otherwise, investors could borrow money in the country with lower interest rates, lend money in the country with higher interest rates, and earn an easy profit on the spread between the two. This is a low-risk transaction if investors can be sure the exchange rate won't change. But borrowing money in one country and lending it in another means selling the first currency and buying the second. This puts downward pressure on the currency with lower rates and upward pressure on the currency with higher rates, making the peg darn near impossible to maintain. When the Chinese yuan was pegged to the dollar, the People's Bank of China didn't have to follow the Fed because capital controls prevented funds from flowing freely between the two countries. By contrast, Hong Kong's central bank follows every Fed move because the Hong Kong dollar is pegged and money flows easily between Hong Kong and the US.

Mimicking another central bank can lead to inflation or other problems if the monetary policy isn't copacetic with the economic environment in the pegging country. Recently, some Middle Eastern countries have faced this scenario as central banks have been forced to cut rates along with the Fed in order to maintain their pegs, despite soaring inflation.

Occasionally, market forces will overwhelm a government, and a peg must be broken. This usually results in a decline in value of the pegged currency—but not always. A broken peg can either cause currency to *devalue*—fall against the currency it was formerly pegged to—or *revalue*—rise against its former pegging partner.

When a currency is devalued, the government might maintain a peg but move the exchange rate. Or it might allow the currency to float. Either way, the exchange rate usually changes dramatically. Table 8.4 shows some of the more well-known currency devaluations,

Table 8.4   Currency Devaluations

Currency	Date Devaluation Began	Total Decline Versus US Dollar
Brazilian real	April 15, 1994	−60%
Mexican peso	December 19, 1994	−53%
South Korean won	October 23, 1997	−53%
Russian ruble	August 14, 1998	−77%
Brazilian real	January 12, 1999	−44%
Argentinian peso	January 7, 2002	−74%

Source: Bloomberg Finance L.P.

including the currency name, the date the devaluation began, and the total drop versus the US dollar.

Sometimes currencies revalue, meaning the formerly pegged exchange rate actually moves up. This is less common because it's easier for a country to maintain a peg when its currency is rising. When a country's currency is devalued, its foreign currency reserves are usually insufficient to maintain the peg. Countries can literally run out of foreign currency reserves while attempting to prop up their currencies. In these cases, sovereign monetary authorities lose out to market forces driving the currency down, so these countries have no choice but to devalue their currencies.

But maintaining a peg when an exchange rate is rising is easier. Countries might run out of foreign currency reserves, but they can't run out of their own currency because they can print as much as they want. So if exchange rates are moving too high, the country can simply print more money. This might lead to a host of other problems, most notably inflation, but it can be done.

Managed Currencies

Some currencies aren't pegged, but they don't float, either. These are known as *managed currencies* (or a *managed float*)—like the Singapore dollar or the Russian ruble. (More managed currencies are shown in Table 8.5). Exchange rates of managed currencies often don't move much more than exchange rates of pegged currencies.

Table 8.5   Managed Currencies

Angola kwanza	Pakistani rupee
Belarus ruble	Russian ruble
Cambodian riel	Singapore dollar
Dominican Republic peso	Sri Lankan rupee
Honduran lempira	Surinam dollar
Laotian kip	Tunisian dinar
Maldivian rufiyaa	Vietnamese dong

Source: Bloomberg Finance L.P.

Countries manage their currencies for the same reasons others peg, and the process of pegging and managing currencies are effectively the same. Governments managing their currencies buy and sell currencies to keep exchange rates within the desired band. But managing a currency is a little easier and allows for more flexibility.

Definition

Managed Exchange Rate

Managed exchange rates are controlled by governments and central banks but to a lesser extent than pegged exchange rates. Managed exchange rates are allowed to move, but only within some predetermined range.

Floating Currencies

Many countries let currency markets determine their exchange rates without much ongoing intervention. These currencies *float*. The currencies of most developed economies float: the US dollar, euro, yen, Canadian dollar, Swiss franc, Australian dollar, and many more. There are some exceptions: Both Hong Kong and Singapore are considered developed economies, yet their currencies don't float. But for the most part, exchange rates for the most commonly transacted currencies are determined by market forces.

Alas, even these governments can't keep from meddling in currency markets entirely. There have been a number of instances when they've intervened, because they thought currencies were either too weak or too strong. A weak currency makes a country's exports less expensive, but it tends to raise the prices of imported goods. The opposite is true when a currency is strong. So countries whose economies are heavily dependent on exports tend to prefer weaker currencies, and big importers often don't mind a strong currency. But neither wants its currency moving too far in one direction.

Governments often work together to impact exchange rates. Moving currency markets usually means buying and selling a lot of currency (or at least threatening to) and using other tools like interest rates, which are most effective in a coordinated effort. In 1985, under an agreement known as the Plaza Accord, several countries combined forces to weaken the US dollar. These same countries then intervened to halt the US dollar's slide in 1987 under the Louvre Accord. Less than two years after it became a tradable currency, the Group of Seven countries (Canada, France, Germany, Britain, Italy, Japan, and the US) intervened to support the euro. Figure 8.2 shows a timeline of currency interventions by major central banks over the years. Note: The euro wasn't officially introduced until 1999, but its value is calculated back further.

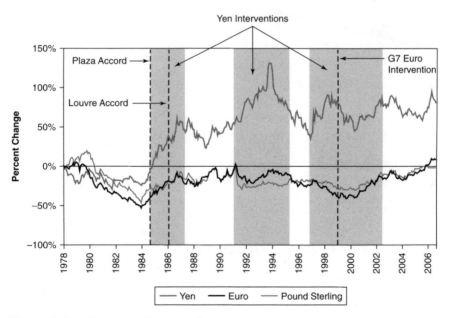

Figure 8.2   Currency Interventions

Source: Bloomberg Finance L.P.; Congressional Research Service, "Japan's Currency Intervention: Policy Issues," (July 13, 2007).

Plaza and Louvre Accords

From the end of 1978 to 1985, the dollar was on a tear against other major currencies. Over that period, the dollar rose almost 70 percent versus the Deutsche Mark, 30 percent versus the yen, and 65 percent versus the pound sterling. The dollar's strength made foreign imports to the US cheap and US exports expensive. The growing US trade deficit became concerning, not only for the US but for other countries as well. The US experienced a recession in the early 1980s, and many blamed a stunted export market. So on September 22, 1985, leaders from the US, Japan, France, the UK, and West Germany met at the Plaza Hotel in New York and crafted a plan to weaken the dollar.

In addition to intervening in currency markets, each country agreed to other measures. The US agreed to lower interest rates while the others raised them. West Germany instituted tax reform. Japan agreed to reform its financial sector. And the US was supposed to cut its budget deficit.

These measures had an immediate impact on the currencies. Within two years, the dollar fell over 50 percent versus the yen and the Deutsche Mark. And the dollar's slide continued even after intervention ceased.

In order to halt the dollar's decline, these same countries signed the Louvre Accord in 1987. This time, the countries worked together to strengthen the dollar, and the dollar stabilized shortly thereafter.

CURRENCIES AND YOUR GLOBAL PORTFOLIO

Obviously, currencies are an important consideration, particularly to global investors. Currencies influence where you can invest because not all currencies are freely tradable. They add diversification to a global portfolio because exchange rates and stock prices tend to have low long-term correlations, which helps reduce risk. (Flip back to Chapter 3 to see how this works.) But most important of all, currencies impact returns.

In the short term, changing exchange rates can add or subtract from foreign stock returns in a big way. In fact, exchange rates can have a bigger impact than the prices of the stocks themselves.

If you own an Italian stock—whether you buy the shares in the US or directly on the Borsa Italiana—changes in the value of the euro relative to the dollar will add to or subtract from that stock's performance when you convert returns back to dollars. If the price of the stock doesn't move but the euro rises 10 percent versus the dollar, the value of the investment increases by 10 percent for a US investor. If the euro falls by 10 percent, the value of the investment follows. If exchange rates move more than stocks, currencies will have a bigger impact on the performance of a global portfolio than stock prices. This happens quite often, as you can see in Table 8.6. This table shows annualized returns on foreign stocks (measured by the MSCI EAFE Index) with and without the currency impact during weak and strong periods for the dollar. From November 1976 to October 1978, a period when the dollar was generally weak, strong foreign currencies increased the return on foreign stocks by 18.0 percent per year (note the local currency returns and the currency impacts don't add in the US dollar returns because they're geometrically, not arithmetically, linked). In contrast, from October 1978 to February 1985, foreign

Table 8.6   Currency Impact on Foreign Stocks

Period Beginning	Period End	Dollar (strong/weak)	US Stocks	Foreign Stocks (in local currencies)	Foreign Stocks (in USD)	Currency Impact
Nov-76	Oct-78	weak	−2.1%	14.0%	37.1%	18.0%
Oct-78	Feb-85	strong	14.2%	16.9%	7.5%	−7.9%
Feb-85	Dec-87	weak	13.7%	20.0%	51.5%	24.6%
Dec-87	Mar-90	strong	17.7%	14.9%	5.9%	−7.4%
Mar-90	Apr-95	weak	11.3%	0.4%	7.1%	6.3%
Apr-95	Jan-02	strong	13.7%	7.7%	1.5%	−5.6%
Jan-02	Dec-04	weak	3.4%	1.0%	14.4%	13.1%
Dec-04	Nov-05	strong	5.6%	25.8%	9.3%	−12.1%
Nov-05	Jun-08	weak	2.7%	2.4%	11.0%	8.7%

Source: Thomson Datastream, MSCI Inc.[6]

currency weakness subtracted 7.9 percent per year from the performance of foreign stocks. The impact of currencies has been greater than the impact of stock prices more often than most realize, especially when the dollar has been weak.

You might be wondering why we bother with stocks when currencies so often do the heavy lifting. There's something to this argument. As mentioned, currencies are liquid, they're easy to trade, currency markets are huge, and they're open all day. In addition, investors can use a lot of leverage in currency markets through the use of derivatives (I'll explain these shortly). So eschewing stocks altogether and trading currencies might not be a bad option—if you're an expert at forecasting exchange rates. But guess what—you're not. Almost no one is. Soros-like success stories in currency markets are few and far between. There are just too many factors at work and too many players involved.

But the good news for global investors: Currencies don't matter much over the long term. Changes in exchange rates have a much smaller impact over longer periods of time. Currencies have added about 0.8 percent per year to a US investor's global portfolio over the last 30 years.[7] That's not insignificant. It's a difference of almost $6 million in cumulative returns on a $1 million initial investment.[8] But it's much, much less than the big swings in performance caused by currencies in the short term. And most of the difference has come in the last few years, thanks to the dollar's recent weakness. Ten years from now, things could look much different.

WHAT'S A GLOBAL INVESTOR TO DO?

Now that your brain is chock-full of currency knowledge, it's time to apply this newfound wisdom to your global portfolio. Here are a few things to keep in mind.

There's No Such Thing as a Free Lunch

Hedging currencies isn't free. The costs aren't extraordinary, but they add up over time. If you spent a mere 0.1 percent of the value of your portfolio every year hedging currencies, you'd have spent almost $275,000 over the last 30 years on a $1 million initial investment! And your performance would have been worse than if you'd done nothing at all.

It's Money Out of the Market

Hedging currency exposure means investing some of your money in the hedge instead of stocks. Stocks make a much better long-term investment than currencies. We said currencies have added 0.8 percent per year to returns on a global portfolio over the last 30 years. Global stocks have walloped those returns, averaging 10.7 percent per year (even without the positive impact of currencies) over the same period.[9] Any money you take out of stocks to hedge currencies will undoubtedly be a drag on your portfolio's long-term performance.

Owning Stocks in a Country Gives You Exposure to That Country's Currency

Owning stocks based in a foreign country provides exposure to other currencies. This might seem obvious and redundant, but it's important enough to reiterate. If you think the dollar is going to be weak, you might consider owning a few more foreign stocks. If you think the dollar is going to be strong, own a few more US stocks.

This isn't a perfect strategy. You run the risk of being wrong about exchange rates. And as you saw in Table 8.6, there have been times when US stocks have done better when the dollar has been weak or foreign stocks have outperformed in a strong dollar environment. But if you're right about the currency, it will provide a tailwind to your portfolio. You get to keep all your money invested in stocks. And your transaction costs won't be much higher than they would be otherwise.

CURRENCY STRATEGIES

Clearly, there are a lot of options when it comes to currencies. But we can distill these down to a few basic strategies for global investors.

Option 1

Forget about stocks and play the currency markets.

We already explained Option 1 requires you to be a currency fore-casting wiz. If you are—go for it! If not, scribble Option 1 out with a black marker and forget I ever mentioned it.

Option 2

Selectively hedge your currency exposure.

This isn't as extreme as Option 1, but you'd still need to know which currencies you should and shouldn't hedge. Make the wrong choices, and you'll not only hurt your portfolio's performance, you'll also pay the aforementioned costs to do it.

Option 3

Hedge all currencies in proportion to your exposure.

If you're going to hedge, this is the way to go. It'll still cost you money. And you have to take some of your investment dollars out of stocks or borrow money to do it and pay a financing fee. But you don't need to know a thing about currency forecasting. Simply hedge currencies in proportion to the exposure in the equities you own. If 10 percent of your portfolio is invested in UK stocks, hedge that amount of currency. You'll have to rebalance your hedges occasionally, but once or twice a year is probably enough.

Option 4

Don't do anything.

I'm not just being lazy. For most investors, this is the best bet. Currencies won't have much impact on your portfolio's performance if you have a decently long time horizon. You get the diversification benefits of currency exposure. You don't have to commit any capital to hedging. And best of all, it doesn't cost you anything!

TRADING CURRENCIES (IF YOU DARE)

If the do-nothing approach isn't for you, and currency trading calls to you like a siren song, you should know something about the vehicles used to trade currencies. These instruments can be complicated and risky because they can involve a lot of leverage. I recommend you get to know the ins and outs of these products in great detail before trading them. But as an initial edification, we've given you some brief descriptions in the following.

Currency Futures

Currency futures are contracts allowing you to exchange one currency for another on a specified date at a specified exchange rate.

Definition

Futures Contract

A *futures contract* is a standardized contract that obliges the buyer to buy some asset and the seller to sell some asset at a set price on some set date in the future. Futures contracts are available on a number of physical and financial assets. You can trade futures linked to commodities, stocks, stock indexes, interest rates, and of course, currencies. Because futures contracts are standardized and they trade on exchanges, they're easy to buy and sell. In the US, currency futures trade primarily on the Chicago Mercantile Exchange. In order to trade currency futures, you must open an account with a futures broker.

Commodities futures are usually settled via delivery of the underlying commodity. If you buy frozen concentrated orange juice futures, you'd better have a big freezer ready unless you plan on selling the contract before the delivery date. Fortunately, most financial futures, such as those on stocks and currencies, settle with cash. When you buy a currency future, you lock in an exchange rate for the period of the contract. If the exchange rate moves in your favor, the value of your contract goes up. If the exchange rate moves against you, the value of your future drops.

Futures involve a lot of leverage because the amount of money needed to buy a futures contract is far less than the amount of currency you get exposure to. The money you have to post is known as the *margin requirement*. This changes as the value of the futures contract changes. If the value of your contract goes down, you must add more money to your account. If the value of the contract goes up, money will be added to your account.

Forwards

Forward contracts are similar to futures, except they're not standardized and don't trade on exchanges. Forwards are contracts directly between two parties. They can be highly customized, but this customization makes them more difficult to buy and sell since a potential buyer would have to want a contract with the terms written into the existing forward contract.

Often, the counterparty in a forward contract is a big financial firm. For them, creating custom forward currency contracts means negotiating the contract terms, providing pricing information, and assuming the risk the investor won't pay up. So unless you've got a huge portfolio, you're not likely to find too many companies willing to write these contacts at a reasonable cost.

Options

Unlike futures and forwards, which involve the *obligation* to buy or sell a currency, *options* give the buyer the *right* to buy or sell. This is an important distinction. If you buy a call option on a currency future, you have the right to buy a currency at a specific exchange rate. If the exchange rate moves up, you can exercise your option and buy the currency at the lower rate. So the value of the option goes up as the exchange rate does. If the exchange rate falls, you're not obligated to do anything, so you can't lose more than you originally paid for the option. This might seem like a great deal, but you usually have to pay the seller of an option a hefty premium for this right.

Mutual Funds and ETFs

There are a growing number of mutual and exchange-traded funds investing in currencies. Most of these are intended to give investors exposure to foreign currencies. Some give investors exposure to a single currency while others provide exposure to a number of currencies. But global investors already have exposure to foreign currencies through their foreign equity holdings. In order to hedge out the currency exposure, a global investor needs an investment that goes up when the foreign currencies fall against the dollar and goes down when foreign currencies are strong. Unfortunately, these options are scarce. You could go short an exchange-traded fund, but this option isn't available in most tax-deferred accounts such as IRAs since they prohibit shorting securities. This strategy also ups your costs because you pay interest on the shares you borrow. And although a few of these funds utilize some leverage, they typically don't use much, so using them to hedge requires committing an exorbitant amount to capital or adding the leverage yourself, which further increases your costs.

The Global View

Managing currencies is no easy task. It can be complicated and even be a drag on returns. For most, understanding how currencies impact the value of a global portfolio is important, but a hands-off approach to currencies is often best.

Ultimately, global investors can view the cash register as half-empty or half-full of currency. The former might include investors with short time horizons for whom changing exchange rates poses some risk. But that risk can be easily managed. For those with longer time horizons, exposure to foreign currencies is a distinct benefit. Most investors' time horizons are longer than they think, so the majority of global investors will fall blissfully into the half-full camp.

9

Common Challenges in Global Investing

Stocks go up and stocks go down. Fortunately, stocks rise more often than they fall, but all investors can expect to experience some of both. This is true for both foreign and domestic stocks. Hopefully, this book has shown you global investing can do many things for an investment portfolio. But going global isn't a cure for the ups and downs of investing in stocks. Shakespeare said a rose by any other name would smell as sweet. Similarly (but much less eloquently), a stock is a stock no matter where it calls home. As outlined in Chapter 3, all stocks have some things in common. So at times, stocks around the world are rising together and at other times they fall together. Global investing can't insulate investors from the whims of the market. Both bull and bear markets often occur globally.

With the risks inherent of investing in stocks in mind, this chapter explores some of the more challenging aspects of global investing. This isn't small print tucked back at the end of the book in the hope you'd already run off to build your global portfolio before reading about the bad stuff. Global investing definitely involves challenges, but so does investing in the US—and anywhere else. The important question is, how much more challenging is investing abroad? Answer: A little, but not nearly as much as most think. One of the main challenges is keeping track of the various markets you're investing in. But overall, the differences between the US and many foreign markets are relatively minor.

The sensational incidents most investors fret about are most common in countries that comprise a small portion of global equity markets. Overthrown governments, currency devaluations, civil war—these events are rare just about everywhere, and extremely rare in developed economies. French President Nicolas Sarkozy is more likely to suffer indigestion from eating bad brie than be overthrown in a bloody coup. And it's highly unlikely German Chancellor Angela Merkel has one too many at Oktoberfest and decides to nationalize German assets held by foreigners. Such events are primarily the realm of emerging countries. And as you read in Chapter 4, emerging markets are growing, but they're still much, much smaller on their own than their developed counterparts. With the majority of your portfolio invested in developed markets, many of the most worrisome aspects of global investing become much less concerning.

Some potentially market-moving incidents will catch you off-guard, but many don't have the impact you think they might. North Korea detonating a nuclear device in October 2006 was a rare event. But even stocks in Asian countries at risk from the fallout (literally) didn't move much. South Korean stocks were essentially flat that month. Japanese stocks managed to rise about 1.5 percent. And stocks in Hong Kong jumped 4.7 percent![1] Uncommon occurrences such as this are almost always unforeseeable, but global investing has been around a long time, so many of the typical perceived risks have been on investors' minds for decades.

Most of the challenges noted here pertain to buying ordinary shares on local exchanges. Some are avoided or at least minimized by using ADRs, ETFs, or mutual funds because they trade in the US. But it's a mistake to think these insulate your portfolio completely. When it comes down to it, investing abroad means owning foreign stocks, even if they're wrapped up in another vehicle. So keep these issues in mind even if you don't hold ordinary foreign shares in your portfolio.

VOLATILITY HAPPENS

Often, global investing naysayers cite foreign market volatility as a reason to stick to the US. They're right about the volatility part, but they're dead wrong that sticking to the US is the answer. Fact is—stocks in individual foreign countries *should be more volatile* than the US. It's not surprising or concerning. As mentioned repeatedly in these pages, the US economy and equity markets are the biggest and most diverse in the world. The diversification here means markets and economic conditions can be less volatile than those in smaller, less diversified countries. But the point of global investing isn't to focus on one, two, or even a few foreign countries. Global investing should be just that—*global*. Realizing the real benefits of global investing requires looking for opportunities in as many countries as feasible so issues affecting any single country shouldn't be more concerning than issues affecting any narrow category of stocks in the US. And as explained previously, these days it's possible to invest in most countries of any economic significance, especially developed countries with the most meaningful roles in global equity markets. So casting a wide net should be the goal of all global investors.

Highly publicized blow-ups like those in Mexico in 1994, Southeast Asia in 1997, and Russia in 1998 raise caution flags. But US implosions have been similarly dramatic. Investors in US technology stocks at the beginning of the century didn't feel much better than investors in Mexico in 1994. From top to bottom, the NASDAQ Index fell almost 80 percent from 2000 to 2003.[2] That's about the same as the drop in Mexican stocks in the early 1990s. From February 1994 to March 1995, Mexico's Bolsa Index lost about 70 percent for US investors (including the declining value of the peso).[3] And losses suffered in US energy stocks from 1980 into 1983 were almost as bad as South Korean stocks from 1995 through 1997 during the Asian Financial Crisis.

Turn back to Table 3.2 and you'll see the US has been the least volatile individual market in the world over the last 30 years. But most US individual sectors have been much more volatile than the US as a whole. Just as relatively volatile individual countries combine for a less volatile global portfolio, relatively volatile individual pieces of the diverse US market combine to make the US less volatile.

Similar to Table 3.2, Table 9.1 compares the volatility (measured by standard deviation) and annualized returns of the 10 US economic sectors to the 10 largest non-US developed markets (these account for about 90 percent of the non-US weight in the MSCI World Index) since 1994, the first year US sector returns are available from MSCI. In some cases, the risk associated with individual US sectors far exceeds the risk associated with individual countries. So saying foreign investing is risky because individual countries can be volatile is no more true than saying investing in the US is risky because technology stocks are volatile. Investors

Table 9.1   US Sectors vs. Individual Countries (1994–2007)

USA Sector	Annualized Return	Standard Deviation	Foreign Country	Annualized Return	Standard Deviation
Consumer Disc	8.00%	17.60%	UK	11.0%	12.8%
Consumer Staples	10.50%	13.90%	Japan	0.1%	19.0%
Energy	17.10%	17.20%	France	12.5%	17.4%
Financials	12.90%	18.60%	Germany	11.9%	21.0%
Healthcare	12.60%	15.40%	Canada	15.7%	18.9%
Industrials	12.10%	15.70%	Switzerland	12.0%	15.8%
Technology	12.30%	29.70%	Australia	13.1%	17.2%
Materials	9.70%	19.90%	Spain	18.4%	20.0%
Telecom Services	4.50%	22.30%	Italy	11.5%	20.2%
Utilities	9.10%	16.20%	Netherlands	11.4%	17.7%
USA	**10.8%**	**14.3%**	**World**	**9.1%**	**13.3%**

Source: Thomson Datastream, MSCI Inc.[4]

should focus on the risk of the overall portfolio instead of the risk of the individual parts.

DOLLARS AND SENSE

Currency is frequently cited as a concern for global investors. Fortunately, you know better. Currencies do represent an additional consideration because they impact returns on foreign investments. But currencies detract from returns on foreign stocks at times and benefit returns at others. The most striking currency risk stems from plummeting foreign currencies, which usually happens during devaluations. This is more of a risk in emerging markets than developed markets. But as explained in Chapter 8, even currencies of developed markets can rise and fall fairly quickly at times. However, the long-term impact is minimal.

Too often, skeptics offer the myopic view that changing exchange rates are risks to be avoided. These folks need to look up their definition of risk—at least as it pertains to investing. Remember, from an investing standpoint, risk means volatility. And a well-diversified portfolio with exposure to many countries and currencies tends to have lower volatility than more narrowly focused portfolios. As highlighted in Chapter 3, this benefit arises from the fact currency impact is minimal given enough time. And currencies and stocks have low long-term correlations. So the primary advantage of having exposure to different countries and currencies isn't better returns, it's less volatility!

POLITICAL RISK

Political risks exist everywhere. In most developed countries, the main risk associated with politics is the potential for dramatic legislative change. Often, big legislative changes mean transferring wealth or power from one group of people and handing them to another. They can also mean creating more onerous regulations or putting governments in control of functions that could be handled more efficiently by free markets. Any of these can cause concern among investors. But these risks are as prevalent in the US as just about anywhere else, so investing outside the US can actually reduce political risk when the winds of political change are blustery here. Still, the often incorrect perception is foreign governments are unstable.

Political turnover happens at very regular intervals in the US. We have presidential elections every four years. Senators are elected for six-year terms, with elections occurring every two years. Members of the House of Representatives are elected for two-year terms, so their elections line up with those for the Senate and the White House. You can set your watch (make that calendar) by the US election cycle.

Other countries don't hold elections so regularly, so their political systems probably seem less sturdy than ours. Since WWII, the average tenure of a Japanese prime minister is only about two years. UK prime ministers have lasted a little more than twice as long, on average. This level of political turnover might be unsettling to some Americans. But a high degree of political turnover is commonplace in many countries. It's usually a reflection of the relatively small amount of real power bestowed on these leaders. Often, the true political power lies in parliament or some other government body where sweeping change is much less frequent than head-of-state changes suggest. For instance, despite the high turnover in Japanese prime ministers, the Liberal Democratic Party and its coalition partners have been in power almost continuously for over 50 years.

Political risk in developing countries can at times be more dramatic. Outright political upheaval is just about unheard of in modern history in developed countries. There hasn't been a *coup d'etat* or similar event in a developed country since 1958 in France when Charles de Gaulle returned to power. But these occur in emerging and frontier markets more frequently. The impacts of such events might be felt in the local market, but global equity markets rarely blink.

One of the more recent coups with any significant impact on equities took place in Thailand in 2006. The Royal Thai Army overthrew then Prime Minister Thaksin Shinawatra in a bloodless uprising. The next day, Thai markets fell almost 15 percent, only to recover most of that loss a day later. Those are meaningful market moves, but Thailand accounts for just 0.2 percent of the MSCI ACWI Index, which represents global stocks including emerging markets. Investors outside of Thailand barely flinched. The MSCI ACWI Index rose 1.2 percent the month of the coup.[5]

Nationalism

Nationalism is one of the more legitimate concerns accompanying global investing.

Definition

Nationalism

Nationalism is a somewhat nebulous term. Essentially, it means putting the interest of a nation ahead of all else, including the interests of foreign investors. From an investing standpoint, nationalism can mean anything from shunning foreign acquisitions or investments in strategic industries to the outright seizure of foreign-held assets. Both are concerning, but the latter is a greater risk to foreign investors.

The US has been guilty of its share of nationalism in recent years. In 2006, members of Congress argued vehemently against a deal that would turn over management of several major US seaports to DP World, a company headquartered in the United Arab Emirates (UAE). DP World eventually bowed to the pressure and voluntarily withdrew from the deal. In 2005, Congress had a similar reaction to the proposed acquisition of Unocal Oil Company by China National Offshore Oil Company Ltd. (CNOOC). That deal, too, was shuttered.

More extreme examples of nationalism have arisen in places such as Russia and Venezuela. Both countries are rich in oil assets, and they're keen on keeping more oil revenue as oil prices have surged. The Venezuelan government has not only taken control of domestic companies to the detriment of their shareholders, it has effectively booted foreign firms from several domestic oil projects in the name of national interest. Russia has done the same. The impact of these events isn't limited to firms in those countries. US-based Exxon Mobil

Corp. has been one of the biggest losers in Venezuela, pulling out of several lucrative projects rather than meeting Venezuelan President Hugo Chavez's demands for dramatically increased royalty payments. And UK oil company BP Plc has slowly been stripped of control of its Russian venture. Frequently, there is little compensation offered to those who lose out in these deals, including equity holders of the affected companies.

Property Rights

Lax property rights go hand in hand with concerns about nationalism. When a government nationalizes publicly held assets, it's disregarding property rights ostensibly in favor of the state.

But property rights concerns go beyond government nationalism. Property rights can also refer to the enforcement of copyrights or patents, the seizure of property, or just about anything formerly owned by one party and swiped by another. So even if the firm you own isn't getting scooped up by a foreign government, its products might suffer if slack property rights affect the firm's products. For instance, it's estimated over half the software peddled outside North America and Western Europe is pirated.[6] Obviously, this has a negative impact on software firms selling in these markets. Lax property rights aren't just bad for individual companies or industries; they can be bad for an entire economy. Without property rights, companies have less incentive to innovate and invest in research and development since they're unlikely to realize the full economic benefits of their efforts. The result is often a less productive economy.

Property rights are a huge issue for countries all over the world, especially as they turn increasingly to emerging markets for growth, as property rights tend to be most questionable in emerging countries.

Taxes

Taxes stink—no matter where you pay them. Not only are taxes no fun, they're also a hassle. Tax issues are tremendously complex, so it wouldn't be prudent to offer any individual tax advice without having examined your books. But there are some taxes that hit virtually all global investors, regardless of their personal situations.

A number of countries levy *stamp taxes* whenever shares are purchased on their exchanges. The UK is one such country. Currently, the UK charges one-half of 1 percent of the value of every share purchased. So buying shares directly on a UK exchange means the stamp tax will add to your transaction costs. The UK has the highest stamp tax on stocks, but other countries use them as well. Hong Kong, China, France, and Singapore are a few other countries levying stamp taxes, albeit currently at lower rates than the UK. One solution to paying stamp taxes on individual shares: Buy ADRs if they're available. Most ADRs are exempt from stamp taxes, so you can avoid the tax by buying the shares right here in the US. As explained in Chapter 7, ADRs often sidestep several of the costs associated with buying ordinary shares (although the ADR might trade at a premium to the ordinary just enough to offset this benefit).

Foreign taxes on dividends and capital gains can be issues, too. The US has tax treaties with many nations to prevent double taxation, but this cozy relationship doesn't exist everywhere. So dividends or capital gains on stocks from some countries might receive more favorable tax treatment than others.

Definition

Double Taxation

Dividends paid by foreign firms are often taxed by their home governments. These dividends are also reported as income for US investors holding foreign shares, so the same dividend income might be taxed here, too. Multiple tax authorities trying to get their hands on your money is known as *double taxation*.

US investors can often claim a credit for taxes paid abroad. And the US has entered into *tax treaties* with some foreign countries in order to prevent double taxation, so you don't pay more in taxes in most of these countries than you would here. The US currently has tax treaties with 56 different countries.

Source: Internal Revenue Service Publication 901.

Capital Controls

Some countries prevent the free flow of capital across their borders. Capital controls can relate to currency transactions, property ownership, and, most importantly for global investors, share ownership. China is the quintessential capital controller. Not only are foreigners prevented from buying most shares on China's domestic exchanges, but China's currency, the *yuan* (aka *renminbi*), can't be freely exchanged either.

Why are capital controls problematic? First, they can affect your access to your assets. If capital controls prevent you from buying, selling, or transferring assets, you might be left without them when you need them. Capital controls can also affect asset values. Generally, illiquid assets are worth less than liquid assets. Imagine you're considering buying shares of two identical companies. Their businesses are the same, their earnings are the same, their managements are the same, and their future prospects are the same. Now imagine the only difference between the two is the liquidity of their shares. One company's shares trade freely, while trading in the other is inhibited by capital controls. Investors will undoubtedly prefer shares of the more liquid stock because it provides them easier access to their assets. So capital controls tend to have a negative impact on the value of an investment.

Capital controls can change any time a government sees fit. Sometimes, controls are eased. China has actually loosened some of its capital controls in recent years, establishing programs allowing more foreign investment capital to flow into China and more investments abroad by Chinese nationals. But capital controls go the other way, too. Following the aforementioned coup in Thailand in 2006, the country enacted controls on stock and currency investments by foreigners. But again, the risk of swiftly enacted capital controls preventing investors from accessing their money isn't a significant concern in developed countries.

RISKS, RISKS, AND MORE RISKS

It's often said there's nothing certain but death and taxes. True, but in investing, risk is possibly the only other guarantee. Here's a look at some more of the common risks global investors face.

Legal Recourse

There's no shortage of lawyers here in the US (insert lawyer joke here), but they might not do you any good if you go to court over an investment abroad. Problems arising with your investments in foreign countries sometimes can't be resolved here in the US. So resolving legal issues associated with overseas investments can mean finding local legal representation and utilizing foreign legal systems, making the process potentially even more expensive and onerous than in the US.

Market Operations

It pays to be aware of operational differences among markets because operational trip-ups can be costly. An example: Settlement periods can differ from country to country. In the US, most stock trades settle three days after a stock is bought or sold. But the settlement period isn't uniform in all countries. In some, it's longer. In others, it's shorter. For instance, trades in South Africa settle five days after the transaction, whereas trades in South Korea, Germany, and Hong Kong settle two days following. If your trade settles before you expect and you don't have cash available *in the right currency*, you could be in for trouble.

Accounting Standards

International accounting has become quite robust. In fact, the Financial Accounting Standards Board (FASB), the organization responsible for establishing accounting standards here in the US, is in the process of harmonizing US Generally Accepted Accounting Principles (GAAP) with International Financial Reporting Standards (IFRS). Already, foreign companies trading in the US can choose to use IFRS instead of GAAP, eliminating the extra step of reconciling the two methods.

Eventually, international standards will be an option for US companies as well. In fact, the Securities and Exchange Commission (SEC) is allowing certain large, multinational US companies to utilize IFRS instead of GAAP starting in 2010. And GAAP could go entirely by the wayside as early as 2014. At present, over 100 countries use IFRS, but not all foreign countries do. So accounting standards can vary widely in countries with different standards, preventing investors from easily comparing stocks in different countries.

Information Risk

Information available on global stocks is easier to get and more reliable than ever. We can thank the Internet for the proliferation of regional, industry-, and stock-related news. But the information we get isn't always perfect. As mentioned in the previous chapter, firms don't always translate their corporate information into English, even in developed countries. Basic news can be difficult or expensive to obtain. And the information you can get your hands on isn't always timely. In fact, many markets are open while you're slumbering, so investors may have already acted on significant information released intra-day well before you're aware of it.

The Global View

It's important to be mindful of the risks, concerns, challenges, and potential pitfalls going along with any investment. Investing in global stocks is no exception. But don't let these challenges cause you to shy away from global investing. In most cases, the perceived risk is greater than the actual risk. And many of these challenges aren't exclusive to foreign companies. US investments face similar issues. A well-diversified global portfolio helps ensure no single risk in a single country causes your portfolio too much harm.

We've come to the end of our global journey—all without leaving your chair (sofa, recliner, bean bag, airplane seat, what-have-you). Your portfolio can now know no boundaries—not by time zone, language, currency, or social custom. The numerous benefits are real as are the unnecessary drawbacks that go along with limiting your investments to any single country.

Hopefully, you're more knowledgeable about what global investing looks like and how to approach it than you were before you first picked up this tome. Learning about the vast benefits of global investing was an important step, but the real leap comes in putting this knowledge to work. Don't be intimidated. Global investing is frequently about as easy as investing in US stocks—and it can be very exciting. There's no reason any longer to be so hampered by the consequences of your origin. Think bigger. Think better! And one day, who knows, maybe you can read a book about intergalactic investing. Think of the return-enhancing, risk-reducing opportunities available then!

Notes

CHAPTER 1: WHO NEEDS A GLOBAL INVESTMENT PORTFOLIO?

1. Global Financial Data; analysis of 20-year rolling periods of the S&P 500 relative to long-term US Treasuries.
2. Thomson Datastream.
3. Bloomberg Finance L.P.; US Department of the Treasury.
4. US Department of the Treasury.
5. Thomson Datastream; MSCI, Inc. The MSCI information may only be used for your internal use, may not be reproduced or redisseminated in any form, and may not be used to create any financial instruments or products or any indices. The MSCI information is provided on an "as is" basis and the user of this information assumes the entire risk of any use made of this information. MSCI, each of its affiliates, and each other person involved in or related to compiling, computing, or creating any MSCI information (collectively, the "MSCI Parties") expressly disclaims all warranties (including, without limitation, any warranties of originality, accuracy, completeness, timeliness, non-infringement, merchantability, and fitness for a particular purpose) with respect to this information. Without limiting any of the foregoing, in no event shall any MSCI Party have any liability for any direct, indirect, special, incidental, punitive, consequential (including, without limitation, lost profits), or any other damages.
6. "The Global 2000," *Forbes* (April 2, 2008), http://www.forbes.com/lists/2008/18/biz_2000global08_The-Global-2000_MktVal.html (accessed July 7, 2008).
7. See note 4.
8. Bloomberg Finance L.P.
9. See note 6.
10. Ibid.
11. Luxembourg Stock Exchange.

CHAPTER 2: NOT AS FOREIGN AS YOU THINK

1. "2007 Production Statistics," International Organization of Motor Vehicle Manufacturers http://oica.net/category/production-statistics/ (accessed June 18, 2008).
2. US Department of Trade and Tariffs.
3. Unilever website found at http://www.unilever.com/ourbrands/personalcare/dove.asp (accessed August 4, 2008).
4. Ibid.
5. Energy Information Administration.
6. "2007's Top 75 North American Food Retailers," Supermarket News, http://supermarketnews.com/profiles/top75/ (accessed October 24, 2008).
7. The Federal Reserve, "Structure and Call Report Data For U.S. Offices of Foreign Entities by Country," (June 30, 2007) http://www.federalreserve.gov/releases/iba/200706/byCountry.htm (accessed June 18, 2008).
8. US Federal Reserve; Structure and Call Report Data for U.S. Offices of Foreign Entities by Country as of June 30, 2007.
9. Standard & Poor's Press Release, "Foreign Sales by U.S. Companies on the Rise, Says S&P," (July 9, 2007).

CHAPTER 3: GETTING MORE FOR LESS: RETURN ENHANCEMENT & RISK MANAGEMENT

1. Global Financial Data.
2. MSCI, Inc. The MSCI information may only be used for your internal use, may not be reproduced or redisseminated in any form, and may not be used to create any financial instruments or products or any indices. The MSCI information is provided on an "as is" basis and the user of this information assumes the entire risk of any use made of this information. MSCI, each of its affiliates, and each other person involved in or related to compiling, computing, or creating any MSCI information (collectively, the "MSCI Parties") expressly disclaims all warranties (including, without limitation, any warranties of originality, accuracy, completeness, timeliness, non-infringement, merchantability, and fitness for a particular purpose) with respect to this information. Without limiting any of the foregoing, in no event shall any MSCI Party have any liability for any direct, indirect, special, incidental, punitive, consequential (including, without limitation, lost profits), or any other damages.
3. Bloomberg Finance L.P.
4. Forbes, (http://www.forbes.com/feeds/ap/2008/04/07/ap4862029.html).
5. Thomson Datastream.
6. Developed/emerging distinction per MSCI classification.
7. See note 5.
8. Thomson Datastream, monthly total returns from 12/31/97–12/31/07.
9. Ibid.
10. See note 5.
11. Ibid.

12. See note 8.
13. See note 2.
14. Thomson Datastream.

CHAPTER 4: THE GLOBAL LANDSCAPE

1. Bloomberg Finance L.P.
2. International Monetary Fund.
3. See note 1.
4. See note 2.
5. See note 1.
6. Ibid.
7. Ibid.
8. Ibid.
9. Ibid.
10. MSCI, Inc. The MSCI information may only be used for your internal use, may not be reproduced or redisseminated in any form, and may not be used to create any financial instruments or products or any indices. The MSCI information is provided on an "as is" basis and the user of this information assumes the entire risk of any use made of this information. MSCI, each of its affiliates, and each other person involved in or related to compiling, computing, or creating any MSCI information (collectively, the "MSCI Parties") expressly disclaims all warranties (including, without limitation, any warranties of originality, accuracy, completeness, timeliness, non-infringement, merchantability, and fitness for a particular purpose) with respect to this information. Without limiting any of the foregoing, in no event shall any MSCI Party have any liability for any direct, indirect, special, incidental, punitive, consequential (including, without limitation, lost profits), or any other damages.
11. "The Global 2000," Forbes (April 2, 2008), http://www.forbes.com/lists/2008/18/biz_2000global08_The-Global-2000_MktVal.html (accessed August 4, 2008).
12. Ibid.

CHAPTER 5: TOP-DOWN INVESTING

1. Thomson Datastream, based on calendar year returns for the S&P 500 from 1926–2007.
2. The MSCI information may only be used for your internal use, may not be reproduced or redisseminated in any form, and may not be used to create any financial instruments or products or any indices. The MSCI information is provided on an "as is" basis and the user of this information assumes the entire risk of any use made of this information. MSCI, each of its affiliates, and each other person involved in or related to compiling, computing, or creating any MSCI information (collectively, the "MSCI Parties") expressly disclaims all warranties (including, without limitation, any warranties of originality, accuracy, completeness, timeliness, non-infringement, merchantability, and fitness for a particular purpose) with respect to this information. Without limiting any of the foregoing, in no event shall any MSCI Party have any liability for any direct, indirect, special, incidental, punitive, consequential (including, without limitation, lost profits), or any other damages.

3. Based on the performance of the MSCI World Financials sector relative to other sectors; Datastream.
4. Thomson Datastream.

CHAPTER 6: FOUR STEPS TO INVESTING SUCCESS

1. Thomson Datastream, as of 12/31/07.
2. About MSCI Barra found at http://www.mscibarra.com/about/ (accessed August 8, 2008).
3. Thomson Datastream.
4. Ibid.
5. The Wilshire News Room found at http://www.wilshire.com/Company/PressRoom/PressReleases/Article.html?article=WARelease030904.htm
6. Dow Jones Wilshire Developed Markets Index Fact Sheet, http://www.djindexes.com/mdsidx/downloads/fact_info/DJW_Developed_FS.pdf
7. About Standard & Poor's overview, http://www2.standardandpoors.com/portal/site/sp/en/us/page.topic/aboutsp_overview/4,1,1,0,0,0,0,0,0,0,0,0,0,0,0,0.html?lid=us_topnav_aboutoverview (accessed August 8, 2008).
8. MSCI, Inc. The MSCI information may only be used for your internal use, may not be reproduced or redisseminated in any form, and may not be used to create any financial instruments or products or any indices. The MSCI information is provided on an "as is" basis and the user of this information assumes the entire risk of any use made of this information. MSCI, each of its affiliates, and each other person involved in or related to compiling, computing, or creating any MSCI information (collectively, the "MSCI Parties") expressly disclaims all warranties (including, without limitation, any warranties of originality, accuracy, completeness, timeliness, non-infringement, merchantability, and fitness for a particular purpose) with respect to this information. Without limiting any of the foregoing, in no event shall any MSCI Party have any liability for any direct, indirect, special, incidental, punitive, consequential (including, without limitation, lost profits), or any other damages.
9. Ibid.
10. Ibid.
11. Ibid.
12. Ibid.

CHAPTER 7: I'M CONVINCED . . . NOW TELL ME HOW

1. Investment Company Institute, "Worldwide Mutual Funds Assets and Flows Fourth Quarter 2007," http://www.ici.org/stats/mf/ww_12_07.html#TopOfPage (accessed August 8, 2008).
2. Thomson Datastream.
3. Ibid.
4. Bloomberg Finance L.P.
5. Investment Company Institute.

6. Ibid.
7. ADR.com.
8. ADR.com.

CHAPTER 8: THE CURRENCY EFFECT

1. "Currency in Circulation: Value," The Federal Reserve Board (March 31, 2008), http://www.federalreserve.gov/paymentsystems/coin/currcircvalue.htm (accessed August 4, 2008).
2. Bank for International Settlements.
3. "Triennial Central Bank Survey for Foreign Exchange and Derivatives Market Activity in 2007—Final Results," Bank for International Settlements (December 2007), http://www.bis.org/publ/rpfxf07t.htm (accessed August 4, 2008).
4. "World Economic and Financial Surveys: World Economic Outlook Database," International Monetary Fund (April 2008), http://www.imf.org/external/pubs/ft/weo/2008/01/weodata/index.aspx (accessed August 4, 2008).
5. See note 3.
6. MSCI, Inc. The MSCI information may only be used for your internal use, may not be reproduced or redisseminated in any form, and may not be used to create any financial instruments or products or any indices. The MSCI information is provided on an "as is" basis and the user of this information assumes the entire risk of any use made of this information. MSCI, each of its affiliates, and each other person involved in or related to compiling, computing, or creating any MSCI information (collectively, the "MSCI Parties") expressly disclaims all warranties (including, without limitation, any warranties of originality, accuracy, completeness, timeliness, non-infringement, merchantability, and fitness for a particular purpose) with respect to this information. Without limiting any of the foregoing, in no event shall any MSCI Party have any liability for any direct, indirect, special, incidental, punitive, consequential (including, without limitation, lost profits), or any other damages.
7. Datastream (calculated by taking the difference between the annualized returns of the MSCI World [USD] and the MSCI World [local] from 12/31/77–12/31/07).
8. Datastream (calculated by taking the difference between $1MM invested in the MSCI World [USD] and the MSCI World [local] from 12/77–12/07).
9. Datastream (annualized returns of MSCI World in local currency).

CHAPTER 9: COMMON CHALLENGES IN GLOBAL INVESTING

1. Bloomberg Finance L.P.
2. Ibid.
3. Ibid.
4. MSCI, Inc. The MSCI information may only be used for your internal use, may not be reproduced or redisseminated in any form, and may not be used to create any financial instruments or products or any indices. The MSCI information is provided on an "as is" basis and the user of this information assumes the entire risk of any use made of this information. MSCI, each of its affiliates, and each other person involved in or related

to compiling, computing or creating any MSCI information (collectively, the "MSCI Parties") expressly disclaims all warranties (including, without limitation, any warranties of originality, accuracy, completeness, timeliness, non-infringement, merchantability, and fitness for a particular purpose) with respect to this information. Without limiting any of the foregoing, in no event shall any MSCI Party have any liability for any direct, indirect, special, incidental, punitive, consequential (including, without limitation, lost profits), or any other damages.

5. Thomson Datastream; See note 4.

6. Amy Thomson, "Microsoft Growth May ebb; Software Pirates Curb Sales," Bloomberg, July 17, 2008, http://www.bloomberg.com/apps/news?pid=newsarchive&sid=aest9kTd5.os (accessed July 18, 2008).

About the Author

Aaron Anderson is a Capital Markets Research Analyst at Fisher Investments where he focuses on global macroeconomic and market trends. Aaron holds BS degrees in Geophysics from the University of California at Santa Barbara and Applied Economics from the University of San Francisco. He writes a regular column for MarketMinder.com titled *The Global View*. Aaron and his wife Kim reside in Danville, CA. They enjoy traveling (and investing) all over the world.

Index